BRF Book Club

Springs of Good and Evil

Leslie Paul

Springs of Good and Evil

Biblical Themes in Literature

Leslie Paul

The Bible Reading Fellowship

First Published 1979

© Leslie Paul 1979

BRF Book Club no. 4

British Library CIP data

Paul, Leslie

   Springs of good and evil. – (Bible Reading Fellowship.
Bible Club No. 4).

1.   Bible in literature   2. English literature – 20th century
– History and criticism

I.   Title
820'.9'3   PR479.B'

ISBN   0-900164-49-2

design/print Eyre & Spottiswoode Ltd

Acknowledgements

The author and publisher make grateful acknowledgement to the following authors and/or executors and publishers for permission to make quotations from the works listed:

Secker & Warburg Ltd and the executors of Thomas Mann for *Joseph and his Brethren*; Heinemann Ltd and the executors of George Moore for *The Brook Kerith*; Eyre & Spottiswoode Ltd and Mr Patrick White for *Voss*; Faber & Faber Ltd and Mr William Golding for *Lord of the Flies, Free Fall,* and *The Hot Gates*; the Wilfred Owen estate and Chatto & Windus Ltd for 'The Parable of the Old Man and the Young' from *The Collected Poems of Wilfred Owen*, edited by C. Day Lewis; Weidenfeld & Nicholson and Mr Saul Bellow for *Herzog*; Hamish Hamilton Ltd and the executors of the estate of Albert Camus for *The Rebel, The Outsider,* and *The Fall*; Michael Joseph Ltd and Mr James Baldwin for *Go Tell It on the Mountain*; David Higham Associates, trustees for the copyrights of the late Dylan Thomas, for 'And Death shall have no Dominion' from *The Collected Poems of Dylan Thomas* published by J. M. Dent Ltd; the Porpoise Press and the executors of the estate of the late Neil M. Gunn for *Morning Tide*.

To Lawrence and Non Paterson
of Madley Vicarage
with the author's love

General Introduction

The second Letter to Timothy speaks of the Scriptures as 'useful for teaching the truth, rebuking error, correcting faults, and giving instruction for right living' (2 Timothy 3:16). This Book Club is a response to the conviction that the Bible still has its uses. It is a book which belongs to the world, universal in its appeal and yet bringing its challenge and message home to individuals and communities in their very particular circumstances. It speaks of a God who is concerned with the world in the totality of its life, and of men and women who are seeking for truth and meaning and finding the end of their search in God. There were those who found the word it brought from God 'sweeter than honey' – and this speaks of the Bible as a book to be enjoyed.

But we may well ask what its continuing relevance is for us today. How are we to use it? The books in the Book Club will be trying to answer questions such as these. To say that it is a book which grips us is to speak of inspiration for life, of a kindled imagination, of a will strengthened and refined for today's decision-making.

The Bible appeals to reason, as we look for a blue-print for living. It appeals to our emotions, as we find ourselves entering the feelings and experiences of the biblical characters, themselves displaying the whole variety of human feelings and aspirations. It speaks to us from despair to despair, from hope to hope, from doubt to doubt, from faith to faith. But, at the heart of the Bible, we have the 'Word made flesh' – a Christ who comes alongside us in the manifold complexities of our human existence. We sense the restoration of purpose, the possibility of light in our darkness, the provision of a goal to be pursued, that we may be 'equipped to do every kind of good deed' (2 Timothy 3:17).

In *Springs of Good and Evil* Leslie Paul takes a look at the way in which some central biblical themes have expressed themselves in English literature. His concern is chiefly with the modern novel, but he indicates, in his opening chapter, that the Bible is a world-shaper. He emphasises the *humanity* of the Bible. 'It is earthiness itself', he asserts; it is full of conflict and violence, leaving no room 'for an amiable and pedestrian religion'. It is because 'its narratives concern humanity in all its situations' that its themes re-emerge in literature. There are the parasitic writers who draw on biblical stories and add their own imagination to them, and their attempts often send us back to the Bible itself for the authentic record. But others portray human tragedy (*The Fall*) or the place of sacrifice in human life (*The Sacrificial Victim*), recognising that safety cannot always be guaranteed and that suffering is fundamental to the attainment of ultimate goals. Some novels may speak of the tormented life which sees in God the enemy rather than the friend (*Rebellion against God*). Dr Paul draws fascinatingly upon the basic stories of a wide selection of books, including the horrific City of Destruction *in Lord of the Flies* and the atheist *Rabbi of Bechev* who finds his peace with God on his death-bed. The concluding chapter echoes the Gospel theme – *Go tell it on the Mountain* – where the message is of a transformed world and a God who is on the side of the men he created.

RAYMOND HAMMER

Leslie Paul

Before the Second World War Dr Leslie Paul was variously engaged in journalism, authorship, and adult education. He served most of his army life in the Army Educational Corps and helped to create the Middle East Forces University in Haifa, as Director of the Modern Studies Wing. In postwar years apart from much broadcasting for the BBC he was successively Director of Studies at Ashridge College of Citizenship and of Brasted Place Pre-Theological College, a Leverhulme Research Fellow, the Research Fellow for the Industrial Society and Research Director for the Church of England and as such author of 'The Deployment and Payment of the Clergy' – the Paul Report.

Until his retirement in 1970, Dr Leslie Paul was lecturer in Ethics and Social Studies at Queen's College, Birmingham and recognised lecturer in Theology at the University of Birmingham. He is the author of many frontier works in theology and philosophy all of which have immensely influenced the rethinking of Christian and humanist positions in recent decades. We instance *The Annihilation of Man, The Meaning of Human Existence, Nature into History, Alternatives to Christian Belief*. His specific contributions to contemporary philosophy are contained in *The English Philosophers* and *Persons and Perception*. He contributes to Bible studies in *The Jealous God, Son of Man,* and *Traveller on Sacred Ground*. And of course his studies of the Church of England are justly famous – *The Deployment and Payment of the Clergy* (the Paul Report), *The Death and Resurrection of the Church,* and the most recent, *A Church by Daylight* (1973).

But he is also, and significantly, a poet and a creative writer. He won the Atlantic Award in literature in 1946 on the commendation of T. S. Eliot. His autobiography *Angry Young Man* gave a title to a whole postwar generation of writers and his spiritual journey, *First Love* has been described by critics as superb.

Such works of highly serious fiction as *The Waters and the Wild* (1975) and the more recent *The Bulgarian Horse* (1979) deal with themes and situations highly relevant to those Dr Paul discusses in this present study – love and compassion, the redemption, and the victim whose innocence makes him the perfect sacrifice.

Contents

1: The Bible as a World-Shaper

How can one speak of the role of the Bible in literature and especially in the novel, without recognising its greatness *as* literature? Here it is without a peer. At the same time one must also acknowledge the Bible as a world document in itself, irrespective of its literary qualities, one of those creations which have shaped the civilised world. Almost at random one may speak of the Vedantas, the Koran and (for my choice) the Dialogues of Plato, Augustine's *City of God,* the *Summa* of St Thomas Aquinas, to name but a few of the documents of this rank. The Bible outreaches them all. No other world-shaping book shows such interest in human history – history as a school for man and a vehicle for God. But the Old Testament, ranging back to the mythical origins of man, and telling the history of the Israelites from fabled beginnings is yet more than history. It tells of man's struggles to reach God, to be sustained by God and yet ready in wilfulness to reject and spurn God. It is a God-haunted book. God is the pivot on which all its records and stories turn, so that Israel and Judah appear as a people who know they are under judgement and their lives are steeled and exalted by this fact. And just because of this effort, generation after generation, to live by the Covenant and under the Law, they become a 'new' people in the world, yielding their story to the whole world in a book of burning intensity.

It is strange to think that the nations which became Christian added Old Testament history to their own. Often they knew more of Israelite history than their own, for their own was simply not documented, and they were more familiar with Adam and Eve, with Saul and David, with Judas Maccabeus and Antiochus Epiphanes than with the fathers of their own nation and its foes.

And so it was that many modern peoples identified themselves with ancient Israelite history. The Boers trekking north from the Cape of Good Hope into the almost empty veldt, escaping what they described as British tyranny, felt themselves to be the people of God fleeing the yoke of Pharaoh, and the American settlers striking westward into a fertile, half-empty continent were strenghtened by a sense of affinity with the people of Moses moving into the promised land. They spoke of their new world as 'God's own country' and without the irony that might attach to the phrase today. Russian Jews today seeking visas for entry into their promised land, Israel, are moved by the consciousness of their 'Babylonian Captivity' at the hands of Russian Communists. Indeed the parallels are legion and the Old Testament has been the handbook of rulers and rebels alike – we have only to recall Cromwell and his Roundheads – and as its stories were read Sunday after Sunday, century after century, in the churches of Christendom, they became, apart altogether from their moral import, the inescapable folklore of every Christian nation. Moses in the bulrushes, Joshua before Jericho, Job with his friends, Jonah and the whale, David harried by Saul, were more real to them than wonders a hundred miles away in their own land. For good measure they named their children after Old or New Testament characters hoping that the biblical virtues of these might be repeated in their offspring. They gave their towns and villages the names of Palestinian originals. (This is certainly the case in the United States.) It is only one significant point that two of the greatest poems in the English language, Milton's *Paradise Lost* and *Paradise Regained,* thunder again the biblical themes of man's fall and redemption and that the greatest single poem in the world, Dante's *The Divine Comedy* is purely Christian. These are still inseparable from the world's conscience. The parables of the New Testament became the folklore of every Christian nation.

What marks the Bible specially *as literature* is not just its history or spirituality but its humanity. It is earthiness itself. In the first few chapters of Genesis, Adam and Eve have been banished from Eden and their first-born, the jealous Cain, has murdered his brother Abel. The *first seed* of Adam has let loose fratricide upon the earth. The story of Cain and Abel is only the first of many Biblical stories of sibling rivalries where murder hangs in the air. This is the reason why Jacob, after stealing the blessing due to his brother Esau, flees away to his uncle Laban in Harran, and why his favourite son, Joseph, was thrown into a pit by his brothers and left, at first, to die. 'When his brothers saw that their father loved him more than any of them, they hated him . . .' 'They plotted to kill him . . .' Just those phrases propel us over thousands of years to the conspiracy to be rid of Jesus of Nazareth. All in all, the Genesis picture is of a savage, unregenerate humanity with flashes of human genius and goodness. Abraham is prepared to sacrifice his son, Isaac, but he is prevented. But how many sons were sacrificed to propitiate the uncontrollable furies of the world and underworld? Thomas Mann, in his epic *Joseph and his Brethren*, has Laban of Harran, brother of Rebecca, kill his first-born son as a sacrifice and bury him under the foundations of his house and we recognise in that the grim, fearful sacrificial practices of those who followed Baal. We have our first picture of a permissive society in Sodom and Gomorrah and of the wrath of God against it, and we have to recall that even at the early time of the Flood, and as justification for it, the Lord 'saw that man had always done much evil on earth and that his thoughts and inclinations were always evil, he was sorry that he had made man on earth.' 'In his sight the whole world had become corrupted, for all men had lived corrupt lives on earth.' He said, 'I will wipe them off the face of the earth.' The violence of man was going to be matched by the violence of God. This is another theme which runs through the whole tempestuous Old Testament story. 'I, the Lord your God am a jealous God. I punish the children for the sins of the fathers to the third and fourth generations of those who hate me. But I keep my faith with thousands [of generations], with those who love me and keep my commandments.'

There is no room in all this for an amiable and pedestrian religion – for something like, say, Confucianism. All is conflict. Love of, and conflict with God, political conflict within Israel, the struggle against Baal, epitomised in the story of Elijah and the hostile priests, the wars for survival against powerful empires, the resistance to the denunciatory prophets, the whole struggle for the soul of Israel in a turbulent society prone to violence. It is all this which makes the Old Testament the epic that it is. It is no wonder that generation after generation of men have read it and seen their own lives and fates mirrored in it. Not even the tender, gentler stories, such as Ruth 'amid the alien corn', the glowing sensuality of Song of Songs, the poetic, spiritual Psalms, the resignation of the agnostic Ecclesiastes – 'I understand that the righteous and the wise and all their doings are under God's control; but is it love or hatred? No man knows' – can affect, though they may relieve, the overall picture of a people in a life and death struggle, calling God to its side.

The New Testament, so totally different in style, content and intention, yet opens in circumstances identical with so many early Israelite dilemmas – that of a nation in bondage to a great empire and awaiting a deliverer and engaged in a dialogue with God about the manner of his appearance and the Kingdom he would inaugurate.

The New Testament does not take over the role of the Old. It does not continue the history of the Jews. It is devoted to the life and passion and teaching of Jesus of Nazareth and the birth of a new religious impulse flying at a tangent from Judaism. From the standpoint of the Old Testament, it is a strange and unwelcome event, and another source of anger, especially about the divine claims made for Jesus. Yet the roots of Jesus went deep into the Old Testament. He was as familiar with it as any devout rabbi and used it as a prophetic instrument which announced his own coming and witnessed to his own role. Indeed he linked himself with the prophetic tradition, saying bitterly that he would be derided and persecuted just as the prophets before him had been.

So much is sweetness and light in the New Testament that one has to remind oneself that it too tells of a tragedy typical of the Old. Its highlights are murders: the murder of John the Baptist, the judicial murder of Jesus, the birth of Christianity itself in the stoning of Stephen, the first martyr, whose death is a sign of the violence Christianity is to call upon itself. And when we reach The Revelation of John and the persecutions are already here, we find that God is assigned again a punitive role against his enemies in the world as terrible as anything called up in the Old Testament.

Nothing in all this denies the loving role of Jesus which casts a glow on the honeyed fields of Galilee where he sat with the simple men who were his disciples and lends enchantment to his parables and to his compassionate and healing encounters in villages and along the roads with peasants, with children and above all with the sick. It is the poetry of his life. But we have to remember the darkness. 'Lord, Lord, why have you forsaken me?' He too was plunged into a quite human desolation in his cruel death. It links him with Isaac looking up at Abraham's knife, or with Joseph beaten and cast into the pit to die, for they too had resurrection.

Yet resurrection does not answer everything. For Jesus is not raised from the dead, like those he himself brought back from death, to continue his life as if nothing had happened, but only to go to his Father in a few weeks, after a few brief encounters with his followers.

Even if he had been raised to a normal life, the Crucifixion could not have been forgotten, for it was no accident, like an illness or a fall; it was a deliberate deed, the doing of the God in man to death. In the Passion therefore one finds an immediate affinity to the tragedies of the Old Testament and the two great books become a unity.

ii

There can be no question of ranging through the Bible in a book such as this to assess its literary merits and to select its most compelling passages. Nor could there be any possibility of analysing literature – it would probably have to be world literature – to trace the effects of the Bible on style and content: a Book so omnipresent diffuses its spirit intangibly; it would be difficult, if not impossible, to pin down. Even to limit the task to the influence of the incomparably beautiful Authorised Version would demand a volume of the size and scope of an Oxford Companion to the Bible, a new kind of commentary in fact! That would be beyond my powers. It may be beyond anyone's powers!

What is to be attempted here is difficult enough. It is to seek out the influence of great biblical themes upon contemporary literature, mostly English, and mostly in the novel of high seriousness. Immediately one is brought almost to a full stop. What creative writer thumbs through his Bible and lights on a passage and says to himself, 'There's a good theme, I'll write about that!' If he did the result would be a sterile, programmed piece of writing. More likely, he, having written his story, would be suddenly thunderstruck by the presence of some great theme from the Bible, the loss of innocence or the face of treachery, say, or the Mosaic law of retribution, an eye for an eye or a tooth for a tooth, or evil heaped upon the good. But I have already said that the Bible is earthy, its great themes are human themes, its narratives concern humanity in all its situations. So even to talk of *biblical* themes is to stretch the canvas intolerably wide. There then would be no limit even to the themes of this exercise, which is intended to be limited. Indeed, there are no models or patterns for this kind of enterprise.

I am forced to proceed intuitively, to feel for the presence of the *mysterium tremendum* in an author's probing of a human enigma, and that is a highly selective undertaking. I am not looking for an author's 'message', though here and there it surfaces, but if I may change the metaphor, for the light that shines *through* the landscape an author is painting, even though he may suppose that he himself is the light shining *upon* the landscape. Therefore, in part, we may be looking at the mystery of the creative act itself and learning that God acts here too. And in that there is a continuity going back to the books of the Bible in which men have always found the hand of the Divine.

The point, however, is to begin and let the theme unfold itself.

2: Bible Stories and Bible Themes

i. Joseph and his Brethren

Yet there is one more stretch of territory to be surveyed, somewhat summarily, before I turn to the main task, and it is a rich territory too. I mean all those works of fiction or biography which are parasitical upon the Scriptures. That is, they draw their themes from the Bible and embroider them, either for moral reasons or simply to gild more gloriously a story already glittering.

I am thinking of such works as Henryk Sienkiewicz's *Quo Vadis*, Lloyd C. Douglas's *The Robe*, or Morris West's *The Big Fisherman*, deservedly best-sellers, or at a higher level *David* by Lord David Cecil. There is a vast literature here made even vaster – as the sands of the sea, even, to use biblical metaphor – if we include biographies of Jesus of Nazareth to which I myself have contributed.[1] To be fair to this literature would demand a separate study, if indeed it could be attempted. I should like all the same to speak of two books in this genre to show its potential, and the pleasure and enlightenment which can be gained from it. The first is Thomas Mann's epic, *Joseph and his Brethren,* a work, by an acknowledged master, of breathtaking scope and audacity – and of authority too – which fills out the bare biblical narrative in a novel in the world class of Tolstoy, Dostoevsky, Proust, Dickens. Perhaps only Solzhenitsyn today has Mann's range, but Solzhenitsyn's novels are often autobiographical[2] and rightly launched with passion against the atheistical Soviet Union and for Holy Russia. Mann, on the contrary, is elegantly above the battle and creates out of nothing, or at least very little, a whole viable Old Testament and Egyptian world, which is of its time and is not ours in fancy dress.

Of course, he could hardly have chosen a more moving theme from the Old Testament. The story has all the constituents of a thriller – the spoilt, effeminate, clever younger son conspired against by his rougher brothers and, though murder was their original intention, sold by them into slavery in Egypt, there to rise to greatness as viceroy and in the end to reveal himself in all his majesty to the once hateful brothers and in revealing, reconciling them to him. Even the moral is built in. Though there are confusions and muddles in the Old Testament story which arise from the different traditions Genesis draws upon (confusion made worse by the Koran, and Jewish and Moslem commentaries) nevertheless it cries out for treatment in a novel. Mann has made it a masterpiece perhaps even towering above *War and Peace* or *The Brothers Karamazov*.

Though Joseph is the 'hero', Jacob, his father, dominates. Thomas Mann has caught the patriarchal figure from the moment that he cheats his twin brother Esau for the birthright and the blessing down to the point where he leads his people Israel into the land of Goshen in Egypt there to greet 'his Lordship my son', long mourned as torn to pieces by wild beasts when he was a lad of 17. Jacob dominates because he is the fulcrum of the story: his love and sacrifice for Rachel – one of the world's most enthralling love stories – are brought to fulfilment with the birth of Joseph, but Rachel is brought to death by the birth of Benjamin during the flight from Jacob's serfdom under Laban. Thereafter everything has to centre on Jacob because all life-lines lead to him, for he it is who determines the hierarchies of the tribal family Israel and even his atrocious favouritism for his most beautiful and intelligent – but vain and prattling – son Joseph is seen by Thomas Mann as the most necessary but mischievous unwisdom by which a hidden but active God works his capricious and often 'heavy-handed' will. God's designs transcend, as Joseph himself comes to accept, the practical good sense of ordinary man in his day-to-day affairs. God's justice is hidden.

Thomas Mann loves what he calls 'the correspondences' of Joseph's story. 'The mind dwells pleasantly upon the marvellous correspondences which history shows: it loves to contemplate the way in which one part is balanced by another part and one scene has its pendant in the next. As once the brothers, seven days after Jacob had received the sign of Joseph's death, had returned from Dothan to mourn with their father and they had been sick with dread how they should find him and how dwell with him under the half false, yet partly true suspicion that they were the lad's slayers: so now, with white among their dark hairs, they were returning to Hebron, with the news that Joseph had not died at all, was not dead now, but living in great glory; and they were almost as weighed down with the task of telling the old man. For uncanny is uncanny and overwhelming overwhelming – whether the content be life or death.'[3]

Yet there is another correspondence to be brought out. Joseph, viceroy in Egypt, with power of life or death over his brothers, as they once held it over him, is full of a confused dread as to how to tell them that he is their brother and alive as presently they would be to tell their father. Mann treats the suspense of all this exhaustingly. But it is the 'pit' which Mann treats as paramount. Joseph is cast into a pit to die. He cannot be held responsible for that. But he is half-guilty in that his self-infatuation, his dream boasting, his vain certainty that everyone must love him more than he loves himself, was even unconsciously calculated to infuriate his brothers as it was certainly calculated to assert his superiority over them. It was the behaviour of a boy of 13 in a youth of 17. Thomas Mann sees his imprisonment in Egypt over the affair with the wife of Potiphar, whose slave he was, as a second descent into the pit. An innocent Joseph? As in the case of the first pit? Yes, but again not without guilt of desire. 'And he longed for her', the Koran says (Sura XII), 'had he not seen a token from his Lord'. The token was a vision of his father Jacob, legend agrees. But even a half-desire seen in the face of so beautiful a youth could set alight the infatuation which brought him to the second pit. He must have known of his power. Thomas Mann exploits this theme with all his genius and gives to Joseph the insight that each (innocent?) fall must be God's will since it leads to higher things. In this he finds the resources for his extraordinary self-confidence which avails him so marvellously in his high office in Egypt, just below the crown.

There are loose ends to the story. They belong to the legend as much as to Thomas Mann. How did the conceited and we should guess ignorant tent-boy from a Bedouin-type tribe, his father's pet, climb to a greatness involving high literacy and mathematical skills in a strange civilised, idolatrous country? One moreover anathema to his father? Why did Joseph never try to escape from captivity to his home (he passed close by on his journey south to be sold)? Why did he never send a message to his father along the Ishmaelite route by which he was spirited away? Thomas Mann does his best, but it remains difficult, just the same, to see in the man Joseph became, the garrulous child naked in worship of the moon as Thomas Mann first displays him.

Thomas Mann breaks all the rules. He addresses, even consults with his readers about what he will put in or leave out. The passage quoted above is such an aside. Then the novel is as much a theologico-philosophical treatise as a work of fiction – an effort to trace God's hand in events – and so, continuously, we have something like Plato's Dialogues in which characters make long set speeches to one another, of a boring and repetitive erudition. (Typically German, this.) Yet Mann's capacity to create characters and to probe depths overcomes these handicaps (products of his own vanity in his prodigious learning?) and so one of the world's best stories triumphs. He weaves a brilliant tapestry of patriarchal, pastoral Israelite society and of Ancient Egypt, which is unforgettable. His tour of the Middle East of those times out-Herod's Herodotus. Put the book on your library list and take it on a holiday. When I put it down I felt a deep sense of loss for an Israel which had become my family too.

---

[1]*Son of Man*, Hodder and Stoughton, 1961.

[2]The exceptions to this statement are immense. He projects a series of historical novels on Russia called *The Red Wheel*. The first, already published, is *August 1914*.

[3]*Joseph and his Brethren* by Thomas Mann, transl. from the German by H. T. Lowe-Porter, Secker and Warburg 1956, p. 1123.

ii. The Brook Kerith

My second book in what I have unkindly called the parasitical – perhaps I should have called it 'derivative' – *genre* is George Moore's *The Brook Kerith*. It is one among a host of books which try to reconstruct the life of Jesus for us by ironing out the inconsistencies and rationalising the improbabilities. Scholarly treatises have of course to work only upon the available evidence and there are hundreds of these, some sympathetic and others unsympathetic to Christian claims, based principally on the witness of the New Testament. But the writer of fiction is allowed to use his imagination and is not bound by evidence. Hence from him, if the book is good, his personal vision is acceptable and can be enjoyed, even if we do not believe him. But his work has to be sincere and self-authenticating. Fiction which is just polemical on the hostile side is as bitter herbs: on the pietistic side it is usually over-honeyed for the critical palate. There are books which err on neither side.

George Moore was, of course, a prominent member of the Anglo-Irish school, centred chiefly in Dublin, which made such a magical contribution to English letters at the turn of the century and beyond. It includes such brilliant figures as W. B. Yeats, George Bernard Shaw, Oscar Wilde, Sean O'Casey, Oliver St John Gogarty, 'A. E.', and many others associated with the Abbey Theatre, Dublin. So we have a right to expect some fine prose from George Moore and we are well rewarded.

Moore presents us with two Christs – the pre-crucifixion wonder-worker and the post-resurrection shepherd. It is his theme that Jesus did not die on the cross, but was thought dead and discovered in a coma by Joseph of Arimathea, then was secretly nursed back to health by him, in a hut in his garden, and eventually hidden in an Essene cenoby in the Judean wilderness where he, Jesus, becomes a shepherd of uncanny skills.

This is how Joseph of Arimathea first sees Jesus, for whom he has been searching for years as the rumoured new prophet upon whom John the Baptist has bestowed his mantle.

'Joseph raised his eyes and saw in Jesus a travelling

wonder-worker come down from a northern village – a peasant, without knowledge of the world and of the great Roman Empire. At every step Jesus's ignorance of the world surprised Joseph more and more. He seemed to believe that all the nations were at war, and from further discourse Joseph learnt that Jesus could not speak Greek, and he marvelled at his ignorance, for Jesus knew only such Hebrew as is picked up in the synagogues. He did not seek to conceal his ignorance of this world from Joseph, and almost made a parade of it, as if he was aware that one must discard a great deal of it to gain a little, as if he would impress this truth upon Joseph, almost as if he would reprove him for having spent so much time on learning Greek, for instance, and Greek philosophy. He treated these things as negligible when Joseph spoke of them, and evinced more interest in Joseph himself, who admitted he had returned from philosophy to the Love of God.'[1]

This 'ignoramus' was preaching, 'in a scrannel peacock voice,' the end of the world: 'the Lord was so outraged at the conduct of his chosen people that he had determined to destroy the world, and might begin the wrecking of it any day of the week. But before the world ends there'll be wars.'[2]

It is an unflattering portrait, of an ignorant fanatic, claiming Messiahship, disowned by his family, and followed by disciples, fearful, poor-spirited, ignorant and credulous out of the backwoods of Galilee and greedy for 'the great share of the world that'll come to them when the prophet returns from heaven in a chariot'.

It is difficult on the basis of that view of Jesus to understand his enormous hold on people and the brilliance and originality of his poetry and parables. Or to make any sense of the love he generates in Joseph of Arimathea, rich and a great scholar, a love so great that Joseph risks his life to save him, nurse him, and hide him from the Roman and Jewish terror among the Essenes in the ravine of the Brook Kerith where Elijah hid and was fed by ravens. (Note the symbolism!)

As a master-shepherd with the Essenes, Jesus recovers slowly from his total amnesia, but can never be fully enlightened as to the events of the passion, for his friend Joseph is killed by Zealots in the streets of Jerusalem – the only living witness to it all. The small, poor, celibate community of Essenes, scraping a living in the hills, fortifying itself against wild beasts and brigands is brilliantly sketched, an achievement the more remarkable because it was accomplished long before our present knowledge of the people of the scrolls. These men are more vivid in their simplicity, piety and honesty than the disciples *The Brook Kerith* presents. The beauty of Palestine and the rigours of its climate come through as poetry. The prose is sheer delight.

Jesus could have stayed in the cenoby and become its president. But the long past events return to him and he has to confess them and a stray guest, Paul of Tarsus, on one of his long missionary journeys, is present and hears them. I leave the story there. There is no gainsaying the skill with which George Moore weaves his story, his fascinating reinterpretation. As a poetic pastoral of Palestine, as a variation on a theme, it is enjoyable and illuminating.

Of course, Moore is not advancing *The Brook Kerith* as the 'authentic' re-interpretation. It is a story, which he, not sympathetic to the Gospel Jesus, would like to believe could be true. And the consequence is that the Essene Jesus is totally credible but it is impossible to accept the early scrawny, sallow Jesus with the scrannel voice and the empty head which Moore conjures up as the wonder-worker in Galilee. The Messiah and the Essene are total contradictions. Jesus could never have become the Essene he is painted to be if he had ever been the deluded impostor he was supposed to be in the first part of the novel.

And so, at the very least, *The Book Kerith* sends us back to its sources, which are our sources too, the Gospels themselves.

---

[1] *The Brook Kerith* by George Moore, Heinemann, 7th (revised) edn 1927, pp. 121–2.

[2] *Ibid.*, p. 117.

iii *Voss* and *Moby Dick*

There is another kind of novel, not precisely biblical, and not parasitical on biblical stories, in which the great biblical themes suddenly and unexpectedly thunder as previously hidden meanings emerge. Such a one is *Voss*, by Patrick White, a novel of Australia of the last century when it was still in part a convict settlement and was divided socially into very distinct and alien social groups – comfortably-off settlers and traders, the ruling Britishers, convicts, freedmen, and the incomprehensible naked aborigines, wary and hostile and living in the mostly unexplored interior of desert and flood. The contrast is vivid between the primitive savagery of the interior, with its inhuman extremes of climate, and the lush Sydney suburb of the well-to-do where the white lifestyle was modelled on Cheltenham or Tunbridge Wells – gardens and picnics on the beach, balls and straitlaced academies for superior young ladies.

This bourgeois paradise is upset by the arrival of a German with the ambition to explore the interior, even to cross the great continent from east to west. It would be incorrect to describe him as an explorer, except in ambition. What evidence there is shows an unhappy man with a youth of restlessness and indecision behind him, with nothing but a knowledge of botany to his credit and an urge to do great and impossible things, to make as it were the North-west passage of the soul. Anything indeed so long as never to be just ordinary! He comes unannounced one Sunday to the house of his principal financial patron, a Sydney business man, and is received by the niece, Laura, since everyone else is at church.

Laura is fascinated and repelled. 'Voss was a bit of a scarecrow.' He easily took offence. His trousers were frayed at the heel. He obviously did not know how to dress. Or how to behave. Out of pride he refuses lunch with the family. He really is a loner. 'How much less destructive of the personality are thirst, fever, physical exhaustion, he thought, much less destructive than people . . . Deadly rocks, through some perversity, inspired him with fresh life . . . But words, even of benevolence and patronage, even when they fell wide, would leave him half-dead.'[1] Henceforth the novel develops a love-story full of a strange symbolism. Laura (herself a sensitive intellectual solitary) and Voss fall in love – a limping, almost adolescent relationship, but spiritually intense. Indeed, when Voss falls ill before his death in the interior, Laura, ignorant of all this, falls ill too with a mysterious fever, and is on the point of death, only to be released when Voss is spared further suffering. They bear the burden of each other's existence 'till death us do part'. Yet their love is unknown to anyone except themselves and they have barely exchanged kisses and a few letters. Laura survives Voss into a spinsterhood spent teaching in an Academy for Young Ladies. After the intense Voss, no one else will do.

Yet this love-story only throws into relief the passion of Voss to make the exploration into the interior come what may, no matter who suffers. He could never have abandoned it for the sake of Laura's happiness! He recruits a ragged band of supporters to accompany him, with almost no thought of their qualifications or staying power: a hero-worshipping boy, Harry, a freed convict Judd; a poet Le Mesurier, a drunkard Turner, a devout but sickly Christian Palfreyman, the ornithologist, and a landowner out for adventure. Two aboriginals are given them as translators and mediators with the blacks. Though the party can hardly be described as disciples, they are all certainly spell-bound by the undoubted charism of the mysterious German. It takes a long time for them to break with his relentless will. Some stay with him to the end. But the beginning of the journey, with its flocks and herds, mules and horses, moving gently through idyllic spring pastures, is reminiscent of the best days of the long journey of the Israelites to the promised land. Indeed someone in the group says that Voss has gone in search of a paradise in the interior, or to found one.

It is a hopeless expedition of incompetents from the very beginning. Their cattle are stolen or die of disease and starvation. Their horses disappear. The mules lie down. They lose precious food when a raft loaded with supplies upsets. They are holed up in a cave one long rainy season, with the plain around turned to marsh and they have very little to eat. The poet writes surrealist verse and falls desperately ill with dysentery. Even Voss, the implacable, for whom sickness and compassion alike are weaknesses falls ill. Yet despite this he nurses and cleans the helpless Le Mesurier who has lost all strength in his fever. For those and related reasons the worshipping white boy saw his tough leader as quasi-divine. 'As the lad stared at his leader, the sun's rays striking the rocks gave the impression that the German was at the point of splintering into light. There he sat, errant, immaculate, but ephemeral, if he had not been supernal.'[2]

There comes a terrible day in the burning desert sun in the landscape of Hell when the starving party find themselves watched by hostile blacks who have already been pilfering their goods. The grim ex-convict Judd wants to shoot at them, Voss to parley – and there is a quarrel. To end it Voss asks the devout Palfreyman to meet the watching blacks. Startled, but always ready in humility to serve, Palfreyman decides to go unarmed and alone, without even the company of the native boy Jackie, who probably would not make himself understood anyway. 'I will trust in my faith,' he declares.

'Palfreyman, who was certainly very small, in what had once been his cabbage-tree hat, had begun to walk towards the cloudful of blacks, but slowly, but deliberately, with rather large strides, as if he had been confirming the length of an important plot of land . . . Both sides were watching him. The aboriginals could have been trees, but the members of the expedition were so contorted by apprehension, longing, love or disgust, they had become human àgain. All remembered the face of Christ that they had seen at some point in their lives, either in church or visions, before retreating from what they had not understood, the paradox of man in Christ, and Christ in man'.[3]

Palfreyman has walked with his palms out-turned in friendship. 'The black men looked, fascinated, at the white palms, at the curiously lidded eyes of the intruder . . . Then one black man warded off the white mysteries with terrible dignity. He flung his spear. It stuck in the white man's side, and hung down, quivering . . .'

A second black rushes upon Palfreyman and stabs him. On his knees, dying, he murmurs, 'Ah, Lord . . . if I had been stronger'. He had failed in faith.

Soon after this the party decided to split up. Judd and two others wanted to go back. Stores were meticulously divided. It is not *called* a mutiny but it is. It dooms them all. Voss, Le Mesurier, the simple-minded boy Harry and Jackie, the grinning aboriginal youth, press on with the now hopeless quest. Then to them disaster also comes when they are taken by a tribe of blacks determined to test white man's magic. They are dying of starvation anyway. Voss, the last one alive, but only just, has his head hacked off on the orders of the tribe by the aboriginal boy Jackie. The Judas-theme is made the more poignant by the fact that a tender relationship had grown up between Voss and this spirited boy. Nothing is spared us in the tragic saga. The boy runs away into the desert and goes mad and dies. Of the party which returned only one, the convict Judd, survived and he by living for many years with a desert tribe as one of them. Laura's recovery, after the severing of her psychic marriage, is the one bright spot.

Years, years later, when Judd has been rescued, a little gone in the head, from the blacks, the dead Voss is being civically honoured for his pioneering by a memorial statue. He was now safe and 'the wrinkles of his solid bronze statue could afford to ignore the passage of time'. Laura is there as one who knew Voss well and with desperate reluctance she meets the once-mutinous Judd who now reminisces about Voss in humility and reverence. 'No. He was never God, though he liked to think that he was . . . He was more than a man . . . He was a Christian such as I understand it . . . He would wash the sores of men. He would sit up all night with them that were sick, and clean up their filth with his own hands. I cried, I tell you, after he was dead. There was none of us could believe it when we saw the spear, hanging from his side, and shaking.' Someone naturally objected to this, since Judd had gone off and mutinied before Voss died and could not know of his death. Judd was unperturbed. 'It was me who closed his eyes.'[4]

What is one to make of this story with its Christian symbolism and civic resurrection? Judd (Judd = Judas?) the one member of the party, a strong man in himself, who never conformed to Voss's will, transforms him into a Christlike figure years after his death, conferring on him the sacrifice that others might be saved made by the humble Palfreyman! True, Voss had tended the sick, had more love in him than he admitted to himself and the love of the faraway Laura was his spiritual support. And the Christian abnegation of the two was amazing. But he was also possessed.

It is very strange, but the actual physical descriptions of him and of his tormented, inner-directed spiritual states closely resemble the portrait (or perhaps caricature) of Jesus drawn by George Moore in *The Brook Kerith*. Jesus was pictured there as a mysterious, scrawny fellow, ignorant and fanatical, pursued like Voss by his compelling demon and exercising a charismatic power over his followers which made them captives of his will. It is the same magnetic influence which Captain Ahab, who confesses to his demonic rage, exercises over the crew of the Pequod in his pursuit of the monster white whale in Melville's *Moby Dick*. That voyage too ended in total disaster. Strangely Captain Ahab is also decapitated, by a tautening harpoon line. And there are sacrificial characters on board the Pequod like Queegneg, the savage harpooneer who when he appeared dying promoted holier and holier thoughts in his shipmates. 'An awe that cannot be named would steal over you as you sat by the side of the waning savage, and saw as strange things in his face, as any beheld who were bystanders when Zoroaster died. For whatever is truly wondrous and fearful in man, never yet was put into words or books.'[5]

Awe is a product of the story *Voss*. The magical desolate interior where natives appear like mirages of dark clouds or forests of still trees is a mysterious tapestry; the reckless motivations of Voss, the clumsy destructive hopes and jealousies of his companions, the death-driven lunacy of it all promotes one, 'beating the brow till the blood comes', to ask *why, why*? What purpose was served? The truly demonic is as awe-inspiring as the veritably saintly and sacrificial, perhaps even more so for the source of holiness in God is easier to grasp than the hidden springs of evil in all of us.

The Vosses and Ahabs of fiction killed their handfuls to

satisfy their demons. But this century has seen their types rise to power over mountains of corpses. *Voss* then produces not just parallels with Christly sacrifice for others, but the warnings of what can happen to those who submit to satanic impulses within themselves and to the societies which approve and encourage them.

Captain Ahab carried unhappily the name of King Ahab whom the prophet Elijah opposed. 'He did more that was wrong in the eyes of the Lord than all his predeccessors [and], more to provoke the anger of the Lord the God of Israel . . .' the first Book of Kings tell us. He it was who through the agency of Jezebel, whose name has come to be synonymous with wickedness, secured the vineyard of Naboth, which he coveted, after his wife had procured Naboth's death through false accusations. Perhaps that was the least of his crimes.

But then the biblical parallels to our century's demonic lust for, and abuse of, power are without number, from the Pharaoh who kept the Israelites as slaves and captives to Herod the Great who sent his soldiers to massacre the babies in Bethlehem. Every effort to probe the divided heart of man, such as Patrick White makes in *Voss*, can be yet another source of revelation to us of the impulses of men even to self-destruction, men for whom power is the greatest drug of all, and who, when they reach its apex find themselves alone and afraid.

---

[1]*Voss* by Patrick White, Eyre and Spottiswoode 1957, p. 21.

[2]*Op. cit.*, p. 263.

[3]*Ibid.*, p. 364.

[4]*Ibid.*, pp. 472–3.

[5]Herman Melville, *Moby Dick; or the Whale,* Penguin English Library edn 1972, ed. Harold Beaver, p. 588.

3: The Fall

i. 'I will wipe them off the face of the earth'
If we take Genesis literally then we are confronted with the
sorry truth that God regretted the creation of man and at the
time of the flood proposed to wipe out the human race. There
is an actual fall of temperature, of hope even, in the early
chapters of Genesis: the man God created to be his companion in an innocent, idyllic world, itself in its beauty a comfort
to God, had escaped control. God had looked upon his creation and found that it was good, and man, made in his own
image, had crowned it. And God, pleased with his work,
rested on the seventh day and made it holy, and the whole
world with it.

Almost on the heels of that, man is cursed by God.

> 'You shall gain your bread by the sweat
>   of your brow
> until you return to the ground;
> for from it you were taken.
> Dust you are, to dust you shall return.'
>   (3:19)

It is an astonishing sequel to the early paean about the
newly created, goodly, Godly earth. What went wrong?
Talking in mythological terms, it is as if God himself made a
mistake. For surely he should have known that a creature
made in God's image was not destined to live a sheep-like life
under a shepherd's total control, but would strike out into
that dimension of freedom in which he could exercise the
dominion with which God had entrusted him. Man eats of
the tree of knowledge of good and evil, against the express
command of God. He is tempted to do so. But that man *could*
be tempted and fall, and for good or ill actually disobey the
God who created him, implies that man possessed the Godly
qualities of freedom and self-will and was exercising them in

his own way. That could be a fall upwards.

We can ask – did God not know what he was doing? But this is the wrong way to put the question. The real question, with which the Genesis writers had to grapple was – how did evil enter into a universe which God had created and over the goodness of which God – and man too – had rejoiced? It could only be seen by those writers as a Fall, even a free fall, from the grace of God in the golden early days of creation. Not a hapless fall, in which one did not know what one was doing, but deliberate, against the will of *God,* as when Cain murders Abel. And that is *sin.* So man, and God, discover evil in the world, and man's culpability for it, which is sin. And this has haunted man, particularly man in the Judaeo-Christian tradition, down to our own time, and will go on doing so, even for those of the liberal tradition who believe that man is inherently good, because the presence of evil in the world *spoils* the world. A world which promises an abundance of truth, beauty, goodness is a world ruined when they cannot be delivered, or are actually destroyed by man. In that perspective man is a flawed creature. All the world's great writers and thinkers seize upon this theme: it has confronted Europe in this century, not only through two great wars and many revolutions, but through two enormous evils, the National-Socialism of Adolf Hitler, and the Communism of Stalin. The West was reluctant to accept the terror they both practised not as a matter of accident but as policy or ideology. 'How could man really act like that, while professing good, in this progressive democratic – even Christian – century?' many asked.

ii.   *Lord of the Flies*[1]

William Golding's novel of this (biblical) title appeared at the end of the first decade after the Second World War when we were still brooding over the enormities the peace had revealed, the living and dead skeletons of Belsen and Auschwitz, the massacres of Katyn, the first incredible accounts of the endless terror, affecting millions, in Stalinist Russia – that hidden world of the Gulag Archipelago which

Solzhenitsyn was to reveal to us. (But then we knew nothing of Solzhenitsyn in the West.) *Lord of the Flies* is a significant touchstone to the brooding of good men on a European holocaust that left us ashen-faced in 1945 and 1946. That *men* should actually have willed this!

Lord of the Flies is at once a simple story of a desert island and an allegory of Eden and the Fall. There is, or has been, a war. A plane in which boys have been travelling is attacked in the air and crashes into a forest on an island. Some, or perhaps most, of the children escape. The grown-ups are killed. A tornado drags the cabin of the plane into the sea, the stranded children are as alone as they could be, scattered and eating fruit in the primitive jungle in a mindless way and suffering the inevitable colic. They are not a unity, not even aware of each other. It is one boy, Ralph, who calls them together.

Who are all these crashed and miraculously uninjured children? They are English schoolboys of twelve and under, but where they have come from and where they were going we are not told. Among them is a cathedral choir school on tour and we do accidentally learn that it has visited Gibraltar and Addis Ababa. But a choir school on tour in wartime? Perhaps the British Council has arranged more curious things! Perhaps the British Council was no more, even then, since an atom bomb had been dropped on the homeland. All the same, whether they were evacuees or boys on some normal home flight we never learn. We are never told the surnames of most of them.

It does not matter. Homesickness is not the great theme it ought to be until their unity breaks down, for the author's purpose is to isolate the boys completely. In the author's hands they are a new creation, tearing off their clothes, naked and innocent in paradise.

'He jumped from the terrace. The sand was thick over his black shoes and the heat hit him. He became conscious of the weight of the clothes, kicked his shoes off in a single movement. Then he leapt back on the terrace, pulled off his shirt, and stood there among the skull-like coconuts with green shadows from the palms sliding over his skin. He undid the snake-clasp of his belt, lugged off his shorts and pants, and stood there naked, looking at the dazzling beach and the water.'[2]

He is in Eden before the birth of Eve, and everything he looked on was good. He stood on his hands presently to celebrate. The boy's dream of a desert island without adults had been realised: the world of *Coral Island* actually existed. The boys themselves speak of this book and of *Treasure Island* and *Swallows and Amazons*.

The boy, Ralph, emerging naked in the Eden, becomes chief of the survivors by virtue largely of his solidity and independence of mind coupled with a half-adult wisdom about their plight and what they ought to do to save themselves. *There has to be a signal fire; they must build proper shelters; they have to avoid defecating everywhere,* and so on and there is first of all an enthusiastic following for this fumbling leadership. But they are inexperienced and ham-handed about everything they do. Their shelters fall down and the signal fire they light burns down half a mountain side and a small boy who is lost in it. There is an almost inexpressible parallel here with the human state. The boys are doomed to futility even when they are willing: their own efforts are not enough: but often they are not willing: they drift off into trivial pursuits or botch things by quarrelling. They are like humanity itself, unable to lift itself out of the quagmire of human nature, and in need of grace.

The boys themselves cry out for a saviour.

' "If only they could get a message to us", cried Ralph desperately. "If only they could send us something grown-up – a sign or something." '

A sign does come. One which is bloody and cynical and eloquent of the hopelessness of the adult world which is really the subject of Golding's fable, a sign of 'the history of blood and intolerance, of ignorance and prejudice, the thing which is dead but won't lie down'.[3]

While the children are sleeping an aerial battle takes place so many miles overhead that it is unheard. A dead pilot dangling from a parachute drifts down over the island finally to come to rest wedged between rocks which overlook the boys' signal fire. His parachute, restless in the breeze, jerks his body backwards and forward, so that he seems alive. His goggles blaze with the reflection of the fire. It is sheer horror. The fire-minders bolt. The signal place is lost.

But even before this event the boys in their exile are divided. Jack, a power-lusting little boy, a demonic, tyrannical leader of the cathedral choir, who boasts he can sing top C, believes he should have been elected leader instead of the sensible, modest and often tongue-tied Ralph. He seizes the opportunity at the beginning to turn his own followers into a hunting pack with painted faces whose hunting lust grows until it is not content with tracking down the island pigs but turns to human sacrifice. An ironic touch, that. The fragile unity of the boys through an assembly which elected Ralph as their chief is finally broken, not only through rivalry between Jack and Ralph, but by the contagious fear about the beast or ghost abroad in the island at night which the gruesome descent of the pilot seems to confirm.

The assembly dissolves in hysteria. The hunting tribe hives off into a vicious dictatorship, which isolates and intimidates its opponents, and draws the waverers to it because it alone can provide meat. In a panic hunting dance Simon, a solitary, religious boy is speared to death. Piggy, Ralph's faithful, intelligent friend, is murdered. Ralph, the elected but now hated chief, is isolated. He is hunted by the painted pack armed with spears. These 'warriors' fire the scrub to smoke him out of his hiding place. Soon the whole island is burning. It has become the City of Destruction.

The doomed Ralph races in panic to the lagoon, his last refuge from an island of ululating boys seeking to kill him. He rolls in the water at the feet of a naval officer, the longed-for rescuer.

'Ralph looked at him dumbly. For a moment he had a fleeting picture of the strange glamour that had once invested the beaches. But the island was scorched up like dead wood – Simon was dead – and Jack had . . . The tears began to flow and sobs shook him. He gave himself up to them now for the first time on the island; great, shuddering spasms of grief that seemed to wrench his whole body. His voice rose under the black smoke before the burning wreckage of the island; and infected too by that emotion, the other little boys began to shake and sob too. And in the middle of them, with filthy body, matted hair, and unwiped nose, Ralph wept for the end of innocence, the darkness of man's heart, and the fall through the air of the true, wise friend called Piggy.

'The officer, surrounded by these noises, was moved and a little embarrassed. He turned away to give them time to pull themselves together; and waited, allowing his eyes to rest on the trim cruiser in the distance.'[4]

[1]Faber and Faber, 1954.

[2]*Op. cit.*, p. 15.

[3]'Fable' in *The Hot Gates* by William Golding, Faber and Faber 1965, p. 95.

[4]*Op. cit.*, p. 248.

iii 'Man produces evil as a bee produces honey'

In 'Fable', in *The Hot Gates,* William Golding has candidly explained *Lord of the Flies*. He accepts his own role as a fabulist and explains that 'by the nature of his craft, the fabulist is didactic, desires to inculcate a moral lesson'. He states his own moral intention.

'Before the Second World War I believed in the perfectibility of social man; that a correct structure of society would produce goodwill; and that therefore you could remove all social ills by a reorganisation of society. It is possible that today I believe something of the same again; but after the war I did not because I was unable to. I had discovered what one man could do to another. I am not talking of one man killing another with a gun, or dropping a bomb on him or blowing him up or torpedoing him. I am thinking of the vileness beyond all words that went on, year after year, in the totalitarian states. It is bad enough to say that so many Jews were exterminated in this way and that, so many people liquidated – lovely, elegant word – but there were things done during that period from which I still have to avert my mind lest I should be physically sick. They were not done by headhunters of New Guinea or by some primitive tribe in the Amazon. They were done skilfully, coldly, by educated men, doctors, lawyers, by men with a tradition of civilisations behind them, to beings of their own kind . . . anyone who moved through those years without understanding that man produces evil as a bee produces honey, must have been blind or wrong in the head.'[1]

Man produces evil as a bee produces honey. But it is the *nature* of the bee to produce honey, not an aberration. So to equate man'a nature with the production of evil, is the most damning indictment of all. What if his evil is not an unhappy by-product of his other qualities, but that for which he was created? Then are we damned indeed. And this is what God is reported as saying in Genesis: 'Now God saw that the whole world was corrupt and full of violence. In his sight the world had become corrupted, for all men lived corrupt lives on earth.' And God confessed to Noah his intention to destroy man and the earth with it. William Golding joins his insights with the Old Testament writers' perception of the fall – the fall on fall – of man. His controlled fury equals theirs. He might have added that God need not bother: man is now equipped to destroy himself. That was the situation reached when he was writing *Lord of the Flies.* The island burning itself out, the paradise destroyed behind the cluster of filthy, sobbing boys on the beach is prophetic. And the rescuing offshore cruiser, beautiful in its tropical trim, is an ambivalent source of salvation. It could itself be destroyed, or be the cause of terrifying devastation in a world which had let loose the atomic furies. The moving last page of *Lord of the Flies* asks – is there any source of salvation left to man?

Golding introduces one visionary among his run-of-the-mill boys on his desert island. His name is Simon. He evinces a need for silence and solitude and prayer even in the lost island among the gregarious, muddled, noisy mob of boys. He singles himself out at the beginning by fainting among the crocodile of choirboys waiting in the sun and is treated with contempt by the leader, the tyrant-to-be, Jack Merridew: 'He's always throwing a faint,' said Merridew. 'He did in Gib.; and Addis; and at matins over the precentor.'

It so happened that Jack's hunting tribe kills a sow and Simon witnesses unseen the hunt and the ferocious blood lust of the kill. The tribe plants the sow's head on a stake near the 'chapel' among the trailing vines where the gently sensitive Simon goes to meditate and from which sacred place he has been watching. The fearful deed, the bloody head, the flies, the heat, the sickness of evil already developing among the boys suck Simon into a trance in which the sow's head speaks with the voice of the devil, the Lord of the Flies, warning him before he falls unconscious (in the moralising accents of C. S. Lewis's devil in *The Screwtape Letters*).

'I'm warning you. I'm going to get waxy. D'you see? You're not wanted. Understand? We're going to have fun on this island. So don't try it on, my poor misguided boy, or else . . . we shall do you.'[2]

And they do. Simon is the outsider, the boy who goes alone, deliberately, and discovers that 'the Beast' sitting on the mountain top is only the rotting corpse of a poor dead airman moved like a puppet in the strings of his parachute. Bearing this liberating news he is caught up in the ritual hunting dance of Jack's tribe and slaughtered like a pig before he can convey it. The prophet is not heard at the moment when his voice might have saved them. From that moment on all is dreadful darkness on the paradisal island. The parallel with the Old Testament prophets who were silenced by stoning is painful.

[1] *The Hot Gates,* pp. 86–87.

[2] *Lord of the Flies,* p. 178.

iv. Desert islands and Utopias

In 'Fable' William Golding makes a bow towards Ballantyne's Victorian classic *Coral Island.* Indeed, the names of two heroes of that story, Jack and Ralph, reappear attached to the central figures in *Lord of the Flies* and perhaps somehow

Peterkin is reincarnated in the hapless Piggy. For the rest there is no resemblance between the two books. Jack and Ralph of *Coral Island* are omnicompetent. They are not lost for ideas or downcast by exile. They have the confidence which marked so many British explorers and pioneers in the eighteenth and nineteenth centuries – that they could not fail: they belonged to a race destined to rule: God was with them. Evil, as William Golding remarked, came to Coral Island from the outside, from cannibals and pirates, who were defeated; it was never the product of the boys' own inwardness. Ballantyne could not have conceived of such a possibility from staunch and brave Christian boys. The painted savage Jack, demonic with blood lust, would have been improbable as well as deplorable. We should not sneer. In their expectations of human nature and in their moral certainties the Victorians – despite all that can be said of them – were more civilised than we are.

Golding turns *Coral Island* upside down. His own desert island boys are shiftless, impractical, scared, cowardly and doomed. Their drift into nakedness is a mark, not of beauty, not of the ideal boy of classical Greece, but of squalor and poverty of spirit. It is a sad thing. But we are dealing with an allegory, a fable, and his boys in their self-dooming through the evil within them are mankind as he sees it in our century. And we can say the same of Ballantyne's boys: for him, though he intended no allegory, they represented the undefeated human spirit, or at least the *British* spirit of his age. The contrast is painful. But of course Golding is all profundity. Ballantyne has none and so he finds none in his boys – they are all surface and that is how his boy-readers wanted it in their hunger for *Boys' Own Paper* adventure stories. Golding was not writing for boys.

All those early desert island stories were success stories. The castaways, treasure-hunters, explorers (always whites), triumph over circumstances, enemies and savages. Crusoe, with his infinite moving patience and contrivance lives to come home. The Swiss Family Robinson conquers in everything through their encyclopaedic knowledge of the Enlightenment of the West. The treasure-hunters of *Treasure Island,* the hero of which is a boy of admirable intrepidity, defeat their mutineering piratical crew. It was not morally in order that good Christian gentlemen should be overcome by such rascals. All this reflects too the spirit of the age.

In our century utopias and desert islands (the utopias of boys) have taken a turn for the worse. *Lord of the Flies* is an example. In it, of course, it is the boys who are evil. In a later desert island story, *The Other Side of the Mountains,*[1] by Michael Bernanos, it is even the earth itself, as well as man, which is evil. An old seaman and a boy survive a cannibalistic mutiny in a becalmed ship somewhere in the Bermuda triangle. They struggle to an island where everything is strange and terrible. The flowers devour human flesh. The trees bow down at dawn to a god deep in a volcano. The rivers gorge on living things. Every human being is slowly petrified or vitrified. The environment itself is poisonous to man – a modern theme indeed. The book ends with this sentence. 'The only memory that remains during the centuries of my life in stone is the gentle touch of tears on a man's face.'[2]

It is interesting to speculate why – in a century of phenomenal human advance – the same pessimism has overtaken the utopias too. Down the centuries men looked forward with hope towards the future societies an increasingly redeemed humanity would build. We may cast back even as far as Plato's *Republic.* Whatever else it promised which we find dubious today, it promised also a just society and argued the case for its achievement. More's *Utopia* was even more hopeful and every successive Utopia, William Morris's *News from Nowhere,* Edward Bellamy's *Looking Backwards,* H. G. Wells's *A Modern Utopia* saw in future times a mankind redeemed from the errors of the past and living a more humane and civilised life. It seemed, when belief in progress was the common denominator of political debate, *to be impossible to think otherwise*.

Our century has, however, rediscovered human evil. Perhaps H. G. Wells himself began it in the last century when, probing into the future in *The Time Machine,* he discovered slave societies. In the end even he preached a kind of human helplessness before a hostile universe in his last book, *The Mind at the End of its Tether*. It was a shock to liberal sensibilities to imagine that the future might be worse than the past and an affront to socialist theories which, whether of the left or right, asserted vehemently the possibility of creating, not the better, but the *perfect* society on the instant.

Socialism, H. G. Wells wrote, 'sees the resources of the earth husbanded and harvested, economised and used with skill for the maximum of result. It sees towns and cities finely built, a race of beings finely bred and taught and trained, open ways and peace and freedom from end to end of the earth. It sees beauty increasing in humanity, about humanity and through humanity. Through this great body of mankind goes evermore an increasing understanding, an intensifying brotherhood. As Christians have dreamt of the New Jerusalem so does Socialism, growing ever more temperate, patient, forgiving and resolute, set its face to the World City of Mankind.'

That was Wells in *First and Last Things*[3] showing at the beginning of the century a millenarian hope only a remove or two from first-century Christianity.

In defiance of that optimism the anti-utopias began to appear. Aldous Huxley's *Brave New World,* George Orwell's *Animal Farm* and *1984* for instance. In all of these the future became doom-laden through the magnification of human evil against which the authors could, on the whole, see only the impotence of goodness. How could goodness be ruthless? How could evil *not* be? It is the story again of the conflict between Jack and Ralph. Ralph's goodness in the end renders him helpless. *Lord of the Flies* is an anti-utopia.

The pessimism of these literary studies is rooted in the image the world has presented today both politically and technologically to thoughtful men. For *Brave New World* is the unstoppable technology of the sorcerer's apprentice overwhelming man and *1984* is the cruel, lying tyrany enslaving man politically and reducing him to a human zero. *Lord of the Flies* sees evil as the prime motivation of man. What a fall is there! But the authors we are discussing were not drawing a bow at random. What they speculated upon

was there – is there – in the world. Tyranny, slavery, geno-
cide, terror, violence and a growing indifference to them
among ordinary people. Hate, injustice, cruelty had – have –
become the common stuff of life. Nineteenth-century France
was brought to the point of revolution by the deadly injustice
to one man, Dreyfus. Hitler slaughtered six million Jews,
Stalin got rid of perhaps twenty million peasants and opponents. No one revolted.

It has been a century calling for prophetic voices. Hence
the writer has so often been given the role of Jeremiah:

> To trample underfoot
>   any prisoner in the land,
> to deprive a man of his rights
>   in defiance of the Most High,
> to pervert justice in the courts –
>   such things the Lord has never approved.
> (Lamentations 3:34–36)
>
> Can the Nubian change his skin,
>   or the leopard its spots?
> And you? Can you do good
>   you who are schooled in evil?
> (Jeremiah 13:23)

---

[1]Gollancz 1969. Michael Bernanos, who died tragically in 1964, was the son of
George Bernanos, author of *The Diary of a Country Priest* and brilliant defender of the
Catholic faith.

[2]*Op. cit.,* p. 107.

[3]Thinker's Library edn 1929, p. 87.

v. Free Fall
'Can you do good, you who are schooled in evil?' could be
the epigraph of another of Golding's novels, *Free Fall*.[1] It is
not, this time, an allegory, but a moral tale, a tale of the Fall,
not in the social context which *Lord of the Flies* so explicitly
creates but in the interior life of a successful artist, Samuel
Mountjoy, whose work hangs in the Tate.

41

The question he asks himself at the beginning of the book is how did he lose his freedom? 'Free-will cannot be debated but only experienced, like a colour of the taste of potatoes. I remember one such experience. I was very small and I was sitting on the stone surround of the pool and fountain in the centre of the park. There was bright sunlight, banks of red and blue flowers, green lawn. There was no quiet but only the splash and splatter of the fountain at the centre. I had bathed and drunk and now I was sitting on the warm edge placidly considering what I should do next. The gravelled paths of the park radiated from me: and all at once I was overcome by a new knowledge. I could take whichever I would of these paths. There was nothing to draw me down one more than the other. I danced down one for joy in the taste of potatoes. I was free. I had chosen.'[2]

Everyone can recall such infantile moments of absolute daring when consciously free of adult presence or control we can do whatever we like (or have the courage to do!) but Golding sets the little incident against a peculiar human impotence, the Pauline confession that 'the good which I would do that I do not, but the evil which I would not, that I do'. This is the un-freedom of Mountjoy's life, in the profound sense of the mystery of his own divided, even unknowable being. At the core of a man sits an 'un-nameable, unfathomable and invisible darkness, always awake, always different from what you believe it to be . . . that hopes hopelessly to understand and to be understood'.[3]

Communication, Golding concedes, is 'our passion and our despair'. Each person, within himself or herself, is a kind of loneliness, not of the cell or the castaway, but of something not directly apprehended in itself, approached indirectly, known indirectly like the sealed-off atom furnace known only by mirrors and indices. Each person is a darkness which communicates with other darknesses. Everyone as Isaiah says is a 'man who walks in dark places' and 'with no light' but not necessarily one who 'trusts in the name of the Lord and leans on his God'. But Golding's sketch of the human person not only makes the communication between one 'darkness' and another dubious and precarious but throws doubt upon the *unity* of every person. A person is perhaps a series of unconnected darknesses and so he cannot possibly know himself. This doctrine, so damaging to human responsibility, would seem to be self-defeating. If every man is a composite of divided and incommunicable isolates, how could one possibly know, and how could there be any common human experiences or common aims?

Yet what Sammy Mountjoy is seeking is more than communication, more even than self-communication, it is redemption and there has to be a known, unitary self *capable* of redemption. And, in fact, a deal of self-recognition goes along with Sammy Mountjoy's struggle to understand how he became enslaved and how he might be freed. His constant questions are 'When did I lose my freedom?' 'How could I have avoided it?' For what he never intended has become the set-piece of his personality.

St Paul pierced to the heart of it: 'It is no longer I who am the agent, but sin that has its lodging in me. I discover this principle then: that when I want to do the right, only the wrong is within my reach. In my inmost self I delight in the law of God, but I perceive that there is in my bodily members a different law, fighting against the law that my reason approves and making me a prisoner . . . Miserable creature that I am, who is there to rescue me . . .? (Romans 7:20–24).

Mountjoy sees himself as a mystery, a misery, a man 'like a stagnant pool' longing to *see* again, as 'clear as spring water' like the little boy he had once been and at that point we begin his life-story which is itself the cry for redemption. And what a beautifully told story it is, in a series of flash-backs as Mountjoy analyses a life become despicable to him and which, despite his protests of numbness, fills him with moral anguish.

He was a bastard brought up in a slum, who never knew his parents. All this is as vivid and authentic as if it came from Dickens, but with an economy Dickens did not often achieve. As a little boy, in response to a cunning friend's dare he commits a sacrilege in a church (he attempts but fails to urinate against the altar), and spits a dry spit instead, is beaten round the ears by the beadle and nearly dies from the mastoid caused by the blows. It is after this incident that Father Watt-Watts, a sad, gentle paedophiliac brings him up, finds him education and bestows on him a self-effacing love which is not returned.

He is persecuted almost to destruction at school by the vicious Miss Pringle. 'She had a crush on Father Watt-Watts – who had adopted me instead of marrying her – and who was slowly going mad.' But it was not just jealousy which made her persecute. She had a brilliant talent for it and enjoyed its execution. Mountjoy called it her religion, and said of her, 'It is a joy to practise one's religion and get paid for it'.

Sammy's life is traced through school life and into art and sex and his falling in love with a beautiful Madonna-like girl called Beatrice (we are intended to remember Dante's passion for the unattainable) who models for the class and with whom he finds it difficult to make contact. Her tranquillity seemed impenetrable. But by the time he has reached his tormented adolescence, he has already rejected morality, which he calls 'conventional' morality, as an imposture. 'Why should not Sammy's good be what Sammy decides?' 'The supply of nineteenth-century optimism and goodness had run out before it reached me.' Sammy's world 'was amoral, a savage place in which man was trapped without hope, to enjoy what he could while it was going'. This was part of his mood when he fell beatifically in love with Beatrice.

Of course, he meets Beatrice again, when they are both students. He is now a man of the world, he thinks, who drinks, whores a bit, is a member of the Communist Party the morals of which over sex are to sleep around when you can and with whom you can. He is in love with the unattainable Beatrice still. Yet he wants to possess her, to compel her to sleep with him, to overcome her distance, her moral and religious misgivings, and bend her to his way. His persistence and bad faith here are reminiscent of the hero of Kierkegaard's *Diary of a Seducer*.

He gets his way. Marriage is only a dream for the future for they are poor students and intercourse not marriage is his intention. 'Step by step we descended the path of sexual exploitation until the projected sharing had become an infliction.' At the end of this sharing 'poor Beatrice bored me. The old magic, the familiar nerve was deadened or burned out.' He has, of course, made her completely dependent on him as a necessary part of his seduction. He has become the centre of her life. What else could conceivably exist now, after her own fall, but life with him? But as she fearfully apprehends his withdrawal, she becomes more dependent, appealing, clinging. Just this bores him more.

He does not know how to break, excepting to cut and run, leaving no message, no forwarding address, confiding nothing to his or her friends. The effect on her is even more shattering than if he had died, for she knows herself contemptuously rejected, insultingly unwanted, thrown aside, her sacrificial love spat upon. Yet she cannot be sure even of this, only that he has gone, without a word. Where? Why? And so to grief is added an unbearable anxiety, a self-accusation too. These icy blasts wither her spirit.

Mountjoy says of himself, 'In all that lamentable story of seduction I could not remember one moment when being what I was I could do other than I did.'

Seven years later – it is the final episode of the book – he is curious to look her up. There are twinges of remorse. He traces her to a mental hospital and gets permission to visit her. It is only after the visit that he learns that she has been there ever since his fatal desertion of her. He used her and doomed her. And in the utter disaster of his visit he is presented with a coarsened, destroyed woman so far gone in madness that death would be the one true haven for her and for whom his visit could be the final shock.

At a point before that he realises the true worth of the Beatrice he had lusted after. 'When I thought back and came on the memory of Beatrice the beauty of her simplicity struck me a blow in the face. That negative personality, that clear absence of being, that vacuum which I had finally deduced from her silences, I now saw to have been full. Just as the substance of the living cell comes shining into focus as you turn the screw by the microscope, so I now saw that being of Beatrice which had once shone out of her face. She was simple and loving and generous and humble: qualities which have no political importance and do not commonly bring their owners much success.'[4]

It is a moving passage which describes how much he has lost and destroyed in Beatrice. Yet it does not explain his Fall into, as Paul would have put it, the captivity of sin. 'What men believe is a function of what they are', Sammy says knowingly to himself at one point, 'and what they are is in part what has happened to them.' But what they are *in the left-over part* is perhaps more important. More perceptively he also says: 'People don't seem to be able to move without killing each other.'

The final truth about his Fall came to him through remembrance of something his head teacher said to him when he was leaving school. 'If you want something enough you can always get it provided you are willing to make the appropriate sacrifice . . . But what you get is never quite what you thought and sooner or later the sacrifice is always regretted.'[5]

What Samuel Mountjoy had wanted above all, even from schooldays, was Beatrice, and to get her he was prepared to sacrifice everything, he admits, even Beatrice herself.

It is the theme of Dr Faustus, of the pact with the devil, selling one's soul to be given the power one wants, and damn the consequences. It is the theme of the predator-seducer scheming to exploit every weakness in the victim so that she will fall in love with that which will destroy her. 'What does it profit a man if he gain the whole world and lose his own soul?' Mountjoy is as much destroyed, a dried husk of a man, as his victim in the end. Graham Greene studies such a man in *A Burnt-Out Case*. It is the theme of Oscar Wilde in *De Profundis* – 'For each man kills the thing he loves . . .' Perhaps above all it is the Judas-theme of betrayal, and with a kiss.

[1]Faber and Faber 1959.

[2]*Op. cit.*, pp. 5–6.

[3]*Ibid.*, p. 8.

[4]*Op. cit.*, p. 191.

[5]*Ibid.*, p. 235.

4: The Sacrificial Victim

i. Abraham and Isaac

The most moving story in the Pentateuch is the intended sacrifice of Isaac by his father Abraham. Isaac was the precious son conceived by Sarah in her old age by the promise of the Lord and now, despite that –

'The time came when God put Abraham to the test. "Abraham", he called, and Abraham replied, "Here I am". God said, "Take your son Isaac, your only son, whom you love, and go to the land of Moriah. There you shall offer him as a sacrifice on one of the hills which I will show you." So Abraham rose early in the morning and saddled his ass, and he took with him two of his men and his son Isaac; and he split the firewood for the sacrifice, and set out for the place of which God had spoken. On the third day Abraham looked up and saw the place in the distance. He said to his men, "Stay here with the ass while I and the boy go over there; and when we have worshipped we will come back to you." So Abraham took the wood for the sacrifice and laid it on his son Isaac's shoulder; he himself carried the fire and the knife, and the two of them went on together. Isaac said to Abraham, "Father", and he answered, "What is it, my son?" Isaac said, "Here are the fire and the wood, but where is the young beast for the sacrifice?" Abraham answered, "God will provide himself with a young beast for a sacrifice, my son." And the two of them went on together and came to the place of which God had spoken. There Abraham built an altar and arranged the wood. He bound his son Isaac and laid him on the altar on top of the wood. Then he stretched out his hand and took the knife to kill his son; but the angel of the Lord called to him from heaven, "Abraham, Abraham." He answered, "Here I am." The angel of the Lord said, "Do not raise your hand against the boy; do not touch him. Now I know that you are a God-fearing man. You have not withheld from me your son, your only son." Abraham looked up, and there he saw a ram caught by its horns in a thicket. So he went and took the ram and offered it as a sacrifice instead of his son.' (Genesis 22:1–13.)

As a reward, as Genesis tells us, God promises that Abraham's seed will multiply until 'they are as numerous as the stars in the sky and the grains of sand on the sea-shore . . . All nations on earth shall pray to be blessed as your descendents are blessed, and this because you have obeyed me' (Genesis 22:16–18).

Isaac has made no protest at all in this attempted human sacrifice so beautifully told and succinctly abandoned as though it had no consequences beyond the 'proving' of Abraham, unless to tell us by parable that the people of Abraham had abandoned the sacrifice of their first-born and first fruits, their primaeval means of propitiating terrible gods, and so broken with the sons of Baal.

But there is another tradition which gives the silent Isaac a voice. He is the willing victim, the consenting partner in the sacrifice which God has demanded. An episode in the Chester Miracle Plays caught this version of Isaac's role, and Benjamin Britten made it into one of the most tender and poignant of Canticles.

'*Isaac:*   Is it God's will I shall be slain?
Abraham: Yea, son, it is not for to layn.[1]

. . .   .

Isaac: Father, do with me as you will,
              I must obey and that is skill
              God's commandment to fulfil,
                  For needs so it must be.
Abraham: Isaac, Isaac blessed must thou be.

. . .   .

Isaac: I pray you father turn down my face
              For I am sore adread!
Abraham: Lord, full loth were I him to kill!
Isaac: Ah, mercy, father, why tarry you so?'

Isaac's loving acceptance of his father's role is made belatedly here in the face of *force majeure,* bound as he is to the pile of faggots and already under his father's knife. It is made after protest too –

> 'Alas! Father is that your will,
> Your own child for to spill
> Upon this hilles brink?
> If I have trespassed in any degree
> With a yard you may beat me;
> Put up your sword, if your will be,
>   For I am but a child.
> Would God my mother were here with me.'

So in this very human and poetic reconstruction of the sacrifice, Isaac's surrender comes as a bow to the inevitable. But suppose he were a willing participant, despite his fears, from the very start? It makes one's heart ache to suppose this, but in a land where the sacrifice of the first-born was practised and the reasons for it were understood, many a first-born son must in childhood have gone in 'fear and trembling' (the title of Kierkegaard's bitter study of the legend) lest this death be required of him. Even if Abraham had not opened his heart beforehand, nevertheless an intelligent boy asked to accompany his fater to a sacrifice in the far distant mountains where sacrifices did not grow on trees and wood was scarce, would be bound to ask questions in 'fear and trembling' when they were without a beast.

Isaac's question need not have been so childishly innocent as the Genesis account makes it sound, nor Abraham's reply so reassuring. God will provide? But then as the boy knew – God, in that land, would demand only that which was most precious as a sacrifice. Something of little value was an insult to God. But that which was of most value was the first-born son, the greatest gift of God. The Series Three Anglican communion service uses the prayer of David in thanksgiving for offerings: it illustrates the theme: 'Yours, Lord is the greatness, the power, the glory, the splendour, and the majesty; for everything in heaven and on earth is yours. All things come from you, and *of your own do we give you.*'

That will have been the spirit in which Abraham set out to sacrifice: that God had a right to take back that which he had given. But it is one thing to be the slayer; it is quite another to accept to be slain, which was Isaac's role. And this subtler reading of the story reverberates with the dread events of Calvary. The whole Christian story, and the theology which explains and justifies it, make the passion of Jesus a willing sacrifice for the sins of the world: 'He is the propitiation for our sins' St John says firmly, and *The Book of Common Prayer* demands the benefits so that 'we and all thy whole Church may obtain remission of our sins, and all other benefits of his passion'.

Yet we have to remember in the death and passion of Jesus – demanded by the populace or fore-ordained by the Father – the agony of Gethsemane, too, and the cry of desolation from the Cross, 'My God, my God, why hast thou forsaken me?' That anguish could have swept over the young Isaac with his father's knife above him, willing though he had thought himself to be.

. . . .　　　. . . .　　　. . . .

The 'sacrifice' and the 'victim', separately and in combination have haunted modern literature perhaps especially since the First World War. We have moved so far from that shattering event that we have forgotten how joyfully some of the young poets sang their willingness for sacrifice and how dreary life seem to many of them without a cause to die for. Thus Charles Hamilton Sorley, who was killed in action in 1915:

> Earth that blossomed and was glad
> 'Neath the cross that Christ had,
> Shall rejoice and blossom too
> When the bullet reaches you.
> 　　Wherefore, men marching,
> 　　On the road to death, sing!
> 　　Pour gladness on earth's head,
> 　　So be merry, so be dead.

That was not written in irony and neither was Rupert Brooke's sequence of sonnets called *1914*.

'Blow out, you bugles, over the rich Dead!
    There's none of these so lonely and poor of old,
    But, dying, has made us rarer gifts than gold.
These laid the world away; poured out the red
Sweet wine of youth; gave up the years to be
    Of work and joy, and that unhoped serene,
    That men call age; and those who would have been,
Their sons, they gave, their immortality.'

Sons again . . .! And that first joyous sacrifice of young men in 1914 gave place, among poets, to the bitterness Wilfred Owen expressed when he took up the story of Abraham and Isaac in 'The Parable of the Old Man and the Young'.[2]

'So Abram rose, and clave the wood, and went,
And took the fire with him, and a knife.
And as they sojourned both of them together,
Isaac the first-born spake and said, My Father,
Behold the preparations, fire and iron,
But where the lamb for this burnt-offering?
Then Abram bound the youth with belt and straps,
And builded parapets and trenches there,
And stretched forth the knife to slay his son.
When lo! an angel called him out of heaven.
Saying, Lay not thy hand upon the lad,
Neither do anything to him. Behold,
A ram, caught in a thicket by its horns;
Offer the Ram of Pride instead of him.
But the old man would not so, but slew his son,
And half the seed of Europe, one by one.'

[1]'Not for to layn' = not to be avoided.

[2]*Collected Poems of Wilfred Owen.* Chatto and Windus 1963, p. 42.

ii. The Fixer

And so it is that both victims and sacrifice have haunted our century. Has there ever been such a century when so many millions have been sacrificed to ideological fixations and

51

fanatical hatreds? I will not rehearse the holocausts and the trail of bones across the world but take one book first as witness to the typical sacrificial victim of our time: it is *The Fixer* by Bernard Malamud,[1] the story of a Jew unjustly executed for the supposed ritual murder of a boy whose blood he is alleged to have drained from his body. Yakov Bok was a Jew from the shtetl in Russia who, about the year 1910, made his way as an odd-job man into a part of Kiev forbidden to Jews and, concealing his Jewishness of course, climbed up until he, an honest and conscientious man, was put in charge of his employers' brickyard and (to his ultimate cost) tried to stamp out the corruption he found there. He is involved in chasing away marauding children, one of whom is ultimately found murdered of 37 stab wounds made by a pointed instrument, which might arouse suspicions, to someone whose mind worked that way, of a special ritual murder. And in Tsarist Russia then, with its crazed anti-semitism, and ferocious Black Hundreds organised as instruments of Christian vengeance against Jews, Yakov Bok has no chance once suspicion is directed against him and it is discovered that he is a Jew. From that moment, not just the local populace is against him but *the whole state* is turned in fury towards him, lusting for vengeance, demanding his execution. He is the typical Jew and according to the loathsome popular prejudice of the times, equivalent to modern racism, what can you expect from a Jew but evil?

The evidence against Bok is such as would be dismissed out of hand were the accused an ordinary Russian. Indeed it is clear that not Bok but the boy's mother and lover, part of a criminal gang the boy threatened to expose, are the murderers. This is not Soviet Russia but Tsarist Russia in which, for all its evils, there is a legal system which is not entirely rigged. A verdict of guilty has to be obtained and if the evidence against Bok is in shreds then a confession must be wrung from him. Bok, in his honesty and single-mindedness, shows a heroic strength and holds the whole state in defiance. He is held in prison for three years before his trial while the authorities try to fabricate evidence against him and to force him to sign a confession.

The conditions are appalling. He is manacled, starved, beaten, tormented to arouse him to resist so that they might have a legal excuse to shoot him, even his food is poisoned so that he might die 'of natural causes'. The lawyer Bibikov, a humane man, defending him, and aware of his innocence, is hanged – lynched – in an adjoining cell. Bernard Malamud tells the story with such power and authority that one flinches from horror piled on horror. How could men do such things? But then — 'man produces evil as a bee produces honey'.

We last see Bok being driven in a coach towards the inevitable hostile trial, still maintaining his innocence. The *cause célèbre* has brought masses into the streets, raging to get at him. The Black Hundreds are everywhere. A bomb is thrown, but Yakov is not killed. He ascends the courthouse steps under guard and there we leave him. To die?

We are reminded of the persecution of Dreyfus, in France, not long before this story, condemned as a traitor because he was a Jew, and of Christ before a jeering mob, ascending to Calvary. Someone said that 'Yakov becomes the moving symbol for all men who were ever the victims of other men's inhumanity.'

What does Yakov say of sacrifice? Chiefly of its uselessness. There seemed no rhyme or reason to what was happening to him. Like Job he questions God. ' "Why me?" he asked himself for the ten-thousandth time. Why did it have to happen to a poor, half-ignorant fixer? Who needed this kind of education? . . . Who, for instance, *had* to go and find Nikolai Maximovitch lying drunk in the snow and drag him home to start off an endless series of miserable events? Was that the word of God, inexorable Necessity? Go find your fate – try first the fat Russian with his face in the snow. Go be kind to an anti-semite and suffer for it.'[2]

He reflected that it was as though the injured Jew the Good Samaritan had helped had been put there by God or Necessity as a trap. No sooner was he found helping him than he was accused of attempting his murder! He should have stayed in the shtetl. 'Yet though his young mother and father had remained all their poor lives in the shtetl, the historical evil had galloped in to murder them there.' No, he concludes, a Jew was not free, nor innocent in a corrupt state, however circumspectly he walked. Rather, he was greedily awaited. The oppressors lay in ambush for him. 'A hand reached forth and plucked him in by his Jewish beard . . . to be the Tsar's adversary and victim; chosen to murder a corpse His Majesty had furnished free; to be imprisoned, starved, degraded, chained like an animal to a wall although he was innocent.' Where was God?

Yakov Bok is a free-thinking Jew, yet does not believe his fate would have been any different had he been a believer. His sacrifice was of no value. Yet when he travelled through the mobs to the courthouse he had become a dignified public person. The civilised world was roused, and trembled for his fate. Tsarist Russia stood condemned whether he lived or died. As with Job, God did not seem to care whom he tested to destruction. Putting Yakov to the test, he tested a world, and above all the Christians in it. Yakov was no more grateful than Job. But perhaps there was in that story what Thomas Mann called the capricious and heavy-handed Will of God to achieve his ends, which were not the ends of man. Then, too, safety could never be guaranteed to any man, however good or exalted, once man himself had let loose evil in the world. This is hard for us to accept today but it was a logic which the Christian martyrs down the centuries steeled, and even to this day steel themselves to accept. Their Master was the first to face it.

[1]Eyre and Spottiswoode, 1966.

[2]*Op. cit.*, p. 330.

iii. Herzog

Moses Herzog, the hero or antihero of Saul Bellow's great novel *Herzog*[1] is a typical bewildered, uprooted American intellectual, only a generation away from his roots in Yakov Bok's ghetto. He is adrift in a society which even before the shock of John Kennedy's assassination, or Vietnam or

Watergate, was itself morally and spiritually awash. He is no victim in Yakov's sense. No one has rigged a criminal case against him and flung him in jail there to be worse off than the vermin in the cell walls. He does not face a death which would draw out his steel or expose his emptiness. He is not a victim of American anti-semitism, at least not noticeably. There is no *special* reason why his life should have crumbled. Yet it has. He summarises it in self-deprecation as 'how I rose from humble origins to complete disaster'.

Moses Herzog is a scholar. He has written a magisterial work on Romanticism which has earned him a world reputation. He has notes for another as searching as the first. 'Romantic individuals (a mass of them by now) accuse this mass civilisation of obstructing their attainment of beauty, nobility, integrity, intensity. I do not want to sneer at the term Romantic. Romanticism guarded the "inspired condition", preserved the poetic, philosophical and religious teachings, the teaching and records of transcendence and the most generous ideas of mankind, during the greatest and most rapid of transformations, the most accelerated phase of the modern scientific and technical transformation.'[2]

He is on the side of the angels. He sees annihilation as no longer a metaphor: good and evil are real. The 'inspired condition' is necessary to all mankind. 'Herzog behaved like a *philosophe* who cared only about the very highest things – creative reason, how to render good for evil, and all the wisdom of old books. Because he thought and cared about belief. (Without which, human life is simply the raw material of technological transformation, of fashion, salesmanship, industry, politics, finance, experiment, automation, et cetera, et cetera. The whole inventory of disgraces which one is glad to terminate in death.)'[3]

So Herzog stands out as the kind of moral philosopher the disintegrating world needs, and a brilliant future awaits him. Yet his own life is in total opposition to his noble vision. He is kind, compassionate, forbearing yet weak and vacillating and his life threatens to crumble into murder and madness. Like Mountjoy in *Free Fall* he is continually asking himself how he fell into this dismal condition and discovering that if you have no scruples and don't mind the price, you can get what you want, and he declares, in the terms Golding uses about *Lord of the Flies,* that evil is power. 'The strength to do evil is sovereignty.' He has not that strength: his goodness is also impotence.

The plot is simple, the human implications immense. Herzog has been married twice: he has a son by the first and a little daughter by the second marriage. He is uneasy with the son but adores the little girl. His second marriage, the key to the book, is with the brilliant, ambitious scholarly Madeleine. He is properly captivated by her beauty and self-confidence, magnificent foils to his fumbling, stumbling nature, just as her elegance is foil to his absent-minded personal disorder.

Does Madeleine love anyone? She just uses Herzog. Once she has all she can get out of him she plans to discard him. She takes his best friend as a clandestine lover and together they plot to eject him from the house he has bought and all his possessions and even to limit his access to his devoted little daughter after the awaited divorce. It is a cold, calculated conspiracy based on intuitions about Herzog's trusting nature. The adulterous conspirators see how easily Herzog's goose-like nature can be exploited to his own doom. Indeed, he is the 'holy fool' and because of the utter demoralisation which followed from the disaster of his ejection from all that he loves it could easily be insinuated that he is not right in the head. And indeed in a way he is not, consumed as he is by a wild grief which cannot comprehend the victory of evil – the utter lack of pity and compassion in the woman he had loved and in the usurping friend to whom he had once confided everything (and who was himself married). It was of Madeleine that Herzog said that evil was sovereign power, and studying a childhood photo of her with that thought in his head, 'She knew more at twelve than I did at forty'.

Dispossessed of home and family and drifting round to doubtful, cheating friends and lovers and would-be lovers in an atmosphere of emotional hungers and psychic fraudulence (a picture of American middle-class society without a parallel) Herzog sinks deeper and deeper into incoherence and instability, his scholarly career, indeed any career, at an end.

He is a young, broken-down *old* man. His more stable brothers are already thinking he needs the care of a mental institution. The endless obsessed letters of protest and justification he writes to everyone, but seldom posts, seem more than eccentricity, rather an incurable state.

The climax of his Lear-like rage and Othello-like jealousy comes when he acquires his father's old pistol and two bullets and goes to shoot the monstrous Madeleine – or the friend-usurper – and himself. Peering through the bathroom window of his lost home he sees the friend-usurper tenderly bathing his little daughter as though she were totally the usurper's own. Herzog is completely unmanned with grief and pity. He abandons the planned murder: perhaps he never meant it. He is then, this completely unlucky man, involved in a car accident in which he and his child might have been killed and faces police charges because he is an armed man. Defeated in everything, disgraced in his daughter's eyes, delivered a sacrifice into the hands of the vicious Madeleine, he nevertheless avoids a mental institution and escapes to live as a hermit in a ruined old family home in deep country among tin cans and rats.

He picks flowers on his first full day there, a beautiful summer day. 'He went around and entered from the front, wondering what further evidence of his sanity, besides refusing to go to hospital, he could show. Perhaps he'd stop writing letters. Yes, that was what was coming, in fact. The knowledge that he was done with these letters. Whatever had come over him during these last months, the spell, really seemed to be passing, really going . . . Walking over notes and papers, he lay down on his Recamier couch. As he stretched out, he took a long breath, and then he lay, looking at the mesh of the screen, pulled loose by vines, and listening to the steady scratch of Mrs Tuttle's broom. He wanted to tell her to sprinkle the floor. She was raising too much dust. In a few moments he would call down to her. "Damp it down, Mrs Tuttle, there's water in the sink". But not just yet. At this time he had no messages for anyone. Nothing. Not a single word.'[4]

The prophet has retreated into the wilderness. To die? To

recover? The world is abandoned either way. The rest is silence. He does not say, 'Let God be their judge'. But it would have been within his character to say, 'Lord, how my enemies have multiplied' when even his psycho-analyst, bewitched by the beautiful Madeleine, turns against him.

. . .   .

The commandment says, 'You shall not covet your neighbour's wife; you shall not set your heart on your neighbour's house, his land, his slave, his slave-girl, his ox, his ass, or on anything that belongs to him.' Madeleine and her adulterous lover coveted everything. When Madeleine decided she could no longer live with her true husband she threw him out of this house by a carefully planned conspiracy and secured a court order that he Herzog was not to molest her. Moses found himself beset by traps which in his innocence he could never have imagined.

The story has affinity with David's pursuit of Bathsheba, where, to secure Bathsheba as his concubine or wife David sends her husband Uriah the Hittite to his commander Joab with instructions that he be placed in the heart of the battle to be killed. And killed he is, 'murdered by the sword of the Ammonities'.

Uriah died. So did Naboth, whose vineyard King Ahab coveted. Jezebel, the queen, framed him with false charges and he was taken outside the city and stoned to death; and the King built new stables on what has once been a good man's flourishing vineyard. So there are parallels again. Ahab inherits through the conspiracy of his consort, so does Gersbach, Herzog's one-time friend, through the machinations of the ruthless Madeleine. We know Ahab's fate: we are not told what Gersbach's turned out to be. To be cheated by Madeleine when she had used him up?

However, may we speak with confidence of Herzog as a sacrificial victim? I am sure Saul Bellow seeks to show him forth as such, not in the sense that Naboth and Uriah died to satisfy the lust of others or Isaac voluntarily faced the knife that Abraham might honour the command of God or Jakov Bok outfaced his persecutors to the very end. Jakov, Uriah, Naboth have the stature of moral giants because of the rank injustice and hatred which surrounded them, against which their innocence shines like gold. 'Evil was sovereign.' Like them Jesus was falsely accused, falsely arraigned, falsely done to death. No man died more innocently, or more painfully, or more ignominiously, naked on a cross, in the burning mountain sun, before jeering bystanders.

It is difficult to speak of Herzog as the sacrificial victim because of the grayness of his fudged world. Truly to represent the triumph of love and goodness one needs the boyhood innocence of Isaac before his father, or of the fat little boy Piggy, who was Ralph's friend in *Lord of the Flies,* before his murderers or the sinlessness of Jesus before his accusers: then the beauty of the pure in heart stands out piteously against stark evil.

Herzog has not that kind of moral fibre. The world he lives in is shabby and compromised. It is the world of the complicated adulteries of John Updike's *Couples* or Mailer's amoral *An American Dream,* where in a sense anything goes if you can get away with it. The victim on whom his own sin weighs heavier than the sin against him of his persecutors is in moral paralysis before the contest begins. He is the scapegoat rather than the victim, driven away to die for the sins of all, including his own, while the wicked stay at home to continue their ways freed now from responsibility for them. He is the very prototype of the afflicted modern man, wounded in his heart by his own sensitive conscience, here like the schoolmaster of Updike's *The Centaur*. In that story the schoolmaster, George Caudwell is 'tormented with the hurt and never to be healed' and begging for death. He is a man seeking redemption and crying like Herzog, 'Oh, for a change of heart, a change of heart – true change of heart'.

It is the eternal biblical cry – Save us from ourselves – but from secular man out of the heart of the dark secular city. Not all the outcry of modern men against the evils of their societies, the tyranny of their own institutions, the injuries they are inflicting on their environment can in the end free them from the cry against their own hearts – which Golding analyses in *Free Fall* with an economy absent from Saul Bellow's rambling and didactic saga.

Of course an age which has demanded so many sacrifices and counts its victims by the millions has a wealth of literature examining all this. One must instance Graham Greene in particular, who, himself a Roman Catholic, has explored the compromised nature of man and the shady side of goodness in numerous novels of such power and insight as to make him the greatest of our novelists. Iris Murdoch, who also explores our complicated dubieties, notwithstanding.

Perhaps it was Simone Weil, in *Waiting for God* and *Gravity and Grace* who made clear to us what affliction means in this age. In her own eyes, her being before God was a *debt* to God, a nothing in its own right, and its ultimate value rested in its total annulment so that it might serve to nourish others – a sacrificial doctrine of complete abandon peculiar to her. Indeed, she not only preached the doctrine of *malheur* or affliction, but lived it. Affliction was for her something which seized the being of the whole person, a slave mark awarded especially to those who most loved God. One sign of it was the capacity, though innocent oneself, to bear the evildoing of others as though it were one's own. Indeed, the innocent and afflicted bore this evil in their souls far more acutely than those who had committed it. The same paradox of the innocence of the guilty and the guilt of the faultless – the deeper the love and understanding the deeper the sense of complicity – haunts Graham Greene's writings too.

So deep did Simone Weil's Gospel sense of the necessity to share the sufferings of others go – 'inasmuch as you do this to the least of these you do so for me' – that when she came to Britain during the Second World War to work for the French resistance she would eat no more than the ration of a French peasant. Taken to hospital suffering from tuberculosis, she still refused food. The verdict on her death was suicide. She was 34, more innocent than any of us and with far less reason for dying, nevertheless her affliction went so deep that she chose to die.

[1] Weidenfeld and Nicholson 1964; Penguin 1965.
[2] *Op. cit.*, Penguin edn p. 172.
[3] *Ibid.*, p. 192.
[4] *Ibid.*, p. 348.

iv. The Heart of the Matter

Major Scobie, of Graham Greene's *The Heart of the Matter*[1]
strangely resembles her in this choice, though he was hardly
an innocent. He emerges in the novel as the just Christian
man, a police chief in a colonial society inherently corrupt
and clouded and confused by wartime exigencies. He is
trusted, even feared, for his uprightness; yet also distrusted,
spied upon because of it, as though all that honesty, to men
less scrupulous, must be a facade for something else. The
reader never loses his belief in Scobie's integrity even while
he watches his reluctant corruption. By Christian and profes-
sional standards, he goes the limit. He commits adultery. He
accepts a loan from the rich and shady Syrian trader, Yusef,
who keeps no written accounts: in what sense is this not a
bribe then? To protect a ship's captain, during his own offi-
cial investigation, he destroys evidence against him. To shield
his wife from knowledge of his own adultery – knowledge,
ironically, she already possesses – he is trapped into smuggling. He is the half-conscious agent of his own native boy's
murder. Finally, he, a believing Catholic, commits suicide. It
would be a formidable catalogue of crime even for one not a
police officer, yet we experience it not as crime but as the
very consequence of integrity.

Scobie is the afflicted one, under sentence like the saintly
but adulterous Sarah in *End of the Affair* or the whisky priest
in *The Power and the Glory,* for whom the love of God,
printed in his very fibres, itself is doom. All that Scobie does
– and does with such clarity of mind – is for love. It begins
with love of his wife which is not in a worldly sense love at
all, but a compassion born of God. He is no longer attracted
to his pathetic middle-aged mate. She is tearful, unhappy, full
of self-pity, even ugly. The climate murders her looks and
her courage. She is literary in a pretentious way. She bores
him and others. She knows herself not to be liked. But this
totality of wretchedness binds him more securely to her than
any passion could. Her piteousness is the very human failure
from which she must be protected. Scobie's love is like a
mother's for a deformed or criminal child; it is the bearing of
the burden of another's existence, come what may, and it

asks no return though it tears him with grief.

It is for this woman who has no sensual appeal at all for him, only revulsion, that he destroys himself. The dubious loan is to pay her passage because she wants to go away. The smuggling is to protect her from an indiscreet letter. Though in mortal sin, and unconfessed, he takes communion with her so that she may not be hurt by his adultery. Even his suicide, though it carries eternal damnation, the utter abandonment by God, he accepts as his duty so that she may be both protected and freed – though as an additional price he has to 'cook the books' – his diary – to make it look like heart failure (and fails here too for this little fraud is discovered after his death). Not even the total loss of the love of God, which he stoically awaits, is able to deflect him from bearing the burden of others. The affliction of everyone is his affliction. He is clear-eyed about it.

'He had always been prepared to accept the responsibility for his own actions, and he had always been half-aware too, from the time he had made his terrible private vow that she should be happy, how far *this* action might carry him. Despair is the price one pays for setting oneself an impossible aim. It is, one is told, the unforgivable sin, but it is the sin corrupt or evil man never practises. He always has hope. He never reaches the freezing-point of knowing absolute failure. Only the man of good will carries always in his heart this capacity for damnation.'[2]

Of course, there is every kind of biblical precedent for sacrifice for others. 'There is no greater love than this, that a man should lay down his life for his friends.' And the sacrifice of God for man is the heart of the poignant Passion Story.

The torn, flawed, self-accusing characters of Graham Greene's and Saul Bellow's novels reproduce themselves endlessly throughout contemporary life and fiction. This to some extent accounts for the nihilism of the outraged young. In the novels of Hermann Hesse, and in particular in *Steppenwolf* (the wild solitary beast of the steppes) doubt is thrown over the existence of the whole man, the unitary personality. Hesse sees man as an amorphous conglomeration of 'states' hardly in communication with each other, which is also Golding's view.

'And if ever the suspicion of their manifold being dawns upon men of unusual powers and of unusually delicate perceptions, so that, as all genius must, they break through the illusion of the unity of the personality and perceive that the self is made up of a bundle of selves, they have only to say so and at once the majority puts them under lock and key . . .'[3] This is one element in the destructive passion of Hesse's *Steppenwolf* – 'I have a mad impulse to smash something, a warehouse perhaps, or a cathedral, or myself, to commit outrages, to pull off the wigs of a few revered idols, to provide a few rebellious schoolboys with the longed-for ticket to Hamburg, to seduce a little girl, or to stand one or two of the established order on their heads. For what I always hated and detested and cursed was this contentment . . .'[4]

And it is fair to say that the debt to the Bible here is beyond computation: no other source is so full of the introspective questioning about the nature of man and his tormented relations with God and his fellows.

Yet there is another element in the stand of Simone Weil in real life and Major Scobie in fiction – the pride by which the angels fell. Their pride is in bearing too much and seeking to accomplish all and when this becomes intolerable to cast their bodies into the grave. Simone helped no one by fasting to death, but indulged her pride. Scobie's desire to play God to his wife, and at the cost of the 'tangled web' of deception to protect her from everything, had spiritual as well as physical death at its terminus. It has only been given to one man, and him we count divine, to bear the sins of the whole world. Both Simone and Scobie had God-given bodies to cherish; without them they could not do God's will in the world. They were not called to cast them away out of spiritual pride.

'Pride goeth before destruction', the book of Proverbs warns, 'and a haughty spirit before a fall'. And Coleridge chided:

'And the Devil did grin, for his darling sin
Is the pride that apes humility.'

[1] William Heinemann, 1948.

[2] *Op. cit.*, p. 60.

[3] Penguin edn, 1978, p. 71.

[4] *Ibid.*, p. 35. Hesse's novel has had enormous influence. First published by I. Fischer Verlag in 1927 I do not think it has been out of print since. Penguin list 14 editions since 1965. However his literary influence is not limited to one novel. See *Beneath the Wheel* and *Magister Ludi* for example.

5: The Rebellion against God

i.   The Blasphemer and the atheist Rabbi

By the waters of Babylon the captive Jews sat down and wept and remembered Jerusalem. They believed themselves a defeated people dying in an alien land. Yet they survived. And it must be said that defeatism was not a characteristic of Israel. Israelites were capable of fighting beyond the point of reason, as when they immolated themselves at the fortress of Masada rather than surrender to the Romans. And from centuries of misfortune disaster and occupation, which should have scattered or even annihilated them, they rose ever more indestructible than ever. Their history in this century must be seen as evidence of this. And for all Jews in the past, though not more than a minority in our time (we are told), their survival as a people would be seen to stem from the covenant with God, which made them a protected nation, a nation itself intended to be a messenger from God to the world.

Yet this intransigent people rebelled against God too, not just against their conquerors and captors. The journey through the wilderness to the promised land is a saga of alternate acceptance and rejection of the saving Jehovah. Even the deliverer Moses, though he triumphs in the end, receives rough treatment, some of it from his nearest and dearest, some of it from God. The episode of the Golden Calf is not a pretty story. There were some who would have given up and gone back to slavery in Egypt.

It goes on, this theme of rebellion, throughout the Old Testament, and into the New. Ezekiel rebukes in the name of the Lord, 'a nation of rebels who have rebelled against me' (Ezekiel 2:3). The prophet Samuel threatens his people that 'If you do not obey the Lord, and if you rebel against his commands, then he will set his face against you and against your king' (1 Samuel 12:15). Job speaks of those 'who rebel against the light of day' and though he is speaking particularly of thieves, robbers and rapists 'the light of day' is the light of God; darkness belongs to evil (Job 24:13). Again and again the warning to Israel comes (as in Numbers 14:9), 'But you must not rebel against the Lord'. All the same he does, and the tribulations of Israel are seen by the prophets as the retribution demanded by God.

> Is Israel a slave? Was he born in slavery?
> If not, why has he been despoiled?
> Why do lions roar and growl at him?
> Why has his land been laid waste,
> why are his cities razed to the ground and
>   abandoned?
> Men of Noph and Tahpanhes
>   will break your heads.
> Is it not your desertion of the Lord your God
>   that brings all this upon you?
> (Jeremiah 2: 14–17)

The very New Testament call to 'repent for the kingdom is at hand' is a rebuke to an apostate Israel seen to have denied its God and stoned its prophets and to be threatened by a new scourging. The theme of rebellion extends even to the angels themselves for Revelation (12:7–9) tells us that 'war broke out in heaven. Michael and his angels waged war against the dragon. The dragon and his angels fought, but they had not the strength to win, and no foothold was left them in heaven. So the great dragon was thrown down, that serpent of old that led the whole world astray, whose name is Satan, or the Devil – thrown down to earth, and his angels with him.'

If angels can rebel, what stops man, whether individually or collectively? After all it was no less a person than Luther who declared that man has a *passion against deity*, he cannot abide deity.

The most faithful and moving explorer of the rebellion against God in an individual sense by modern man is the Yiddish writer, Isaac Bashevis Singer, winner of the Nobel prize for Literature in 1977, and himself a devoutly religious man weaned in the Hasidic tradition of Eastern Europe. He has many profound and revealing studies of Jewishness in the ghettoes of Europe and New York and from them I choose two characters who reveal the nature of Jewish atheism – the Rabbi Nechemiah of Bechev and Chazkele the Blasphemer.[1]

Chazkele, called 'Chazkele the Bastard' because he did not resemble his siblings, had a chip on his shoulder from his childhood in a poverty-stricken Jewish village in Poland. He was always being beaten at home for some malicious misdemeanour or threatened at school for the insolence of his intelligent objections to his bland, formal and mindless instruction. Not just his fellow Jews, but God himself he called into question. 'Even in cheder, Chazkele began to ask questions about God. If God is merciful, why do small children die? If he loves the Jews, why do the Gentiles beat them? If he is the Father of all creatures, why does he allow the cat to kill the mouse?'[2]

He refused *bar mitzvah,* that ceremony which delightfully recognises and distinguishes every Jewish boy at puberty, and of course got a beating, on one occasion till he lost consciousness. He 'stole books from the study house and went to read them in the women's section of the synagogue, which was empty all week long. When something in a book didn't please him, he erased the words with a pencil or he tore out a page. Once he was caught tearing out a page and from then on he wasn't permitted to enter the study house . . . Chazkele was as good as excommunicated. He threw off the yoke of Jewishness completely.'[3] He even defiled the Ark.

His father's ancient and starving nag, on which the family's livelihood depended, had died just before that senseless blasphemy. 'It lay with its protruding ribs in front of the stable, wet with sweat, salivating, urinating, heaving its sides.' Chazkele and his father, indeed the whole family, wept.

When caught and challenged over the defiling of the Ark with horse dung and a dead mouse, he confessed. But what was the sense of it? the rabbi cried. 'And Chazkele said, "A God who can so torture an innocent nag is a murderer not a God". He spat and cried. He spoke such words that the rabbi's wife had to stop her ears.'

The child of such furious anguish and petty spite against God was driven from town, an outcast, an Ishmael. He ended up in Warsaw in bad company but refused to join thieves because 'one should live honestly', or the terrorists who seek to assassinate the Czar because 'Is it the czar's fault that he was born a czar? Are the rich to blame for being lucky? Would you throw away money if you had it?' He had indeed an answer for everything, even the Christian missionaries who sought to convert him. 'If Jesus is the Messiah, then why is the world full of evil? And if God can have a son, why can't he have a daughter?'

The whole of his life in Warsaw was a disaster almost wholly brought on by his refusal to conform to all the accepted hypocrisies, and even to the accepted decencies! When he refused to have his newborn child circumcised according to the law, a mob smashed the windows of his house with hammers and broke in to bring about the circumcision by force.

Dying in hospital Chazkele behaves so scandalously that he was nearly thrown out. He did not want a customary burial but demands that his dead body should be cut up and thrown to the dogs. Instead, ironically, he was given a formal Jewish burial with his five-year-old son reciting Kaddish at the grave.

'Who listens to a madman?' the narrator asks.

A madman? Just that? If madness, it is the madness of a man pursued by the Furies who give him no inward peace. Neither he himself, nor the world is to be borne. The world is a place of horror, cruelty, lies, pain, death, hardly the handiwork of a loving creator. He is entitled to hate himself for his share in its evil. This is his sad *raison d'etre*. We are invited to mourn him, who understood neither himself nor the world but had taken the measure of the wickedness of his fellowmen.

And the same sadness overhangs the life and death of Singer's Rabbi Nechemiah of Bechev, a man living a life of Franciscan poverty in his dying hamlet, who in middle years, like Dante, finds himself lost in a dark wood. He can no longer believe in that in which all his life he has taught. It is not just despairing agnosticism by which he is afflicted, but wrath against the Creator.

'Yes, you are great, eternal, all mighty, wise, even full of mercy. But with whom do you play hide-and-seek – with flies? What help is your greatness to the fly when it falls into the web of the spider that sucks out its life? Of what avail are all your attributes to the mouse when the cat clamps it in its claws? Rewards in Paradise? The beasts have no use for them. You, Father in heaven, have the time to wait for the end of days, but they can't wait.'[4]

Afflicted like Job, he dreams the most terrible dreams – of Jews being burned at the stake, of schoolboys being strung-up on the gallows, of young girls violated, of tortured infants and babies impaled on Cossack spears and buried while they were still alive. 'In his dream the rabbi waved his fist towards heaven and shouted, "Is all this for your glory, Heavenly Killer?" '

Like Chazkele, the Rabbi flees to Warsaw, but stealthily, without a word, leaving his post and scattering alarm and confusion behind him. He will seek answers to his fury, even Gentile answers. But Warsaw is sheer hell to him, he is the innocent abroad trying to find his way through a maze of crime and corruption. Defeated both in his own soul and in search for truth he returns to Bechev to die.

On his death-bed God returns to him. He 'lay down on his bed fully clothed. He felt his strength leaving him – not ebbing away but all at once, rapidly. A light he never knew was there flickered in his brain. His hands and feet grew numb. His head lay heavy on the pillow. After a time, the rabbi lifted an eyelid. The candle had burned out. A pre-dawn moon, jagged and dimmed by fog, shone through the window. In the east, the sky reddened. "Something is there," the rabbi murmured.

'The war between the rabbi of Bechev and God had come to an end'[5]

---

[1]Both are to be found in English translation in a collection of short stories by Isaac Bashevis Singer, *A Friend of Kafka*, Jonathan Cape, 1972. The Rabbi is in 'Something is There', p. 283 to end of the book and Chazkele is in 'The Blasphemer' p. 219 *et seq*. It must be said that Singer is a great humorist too. Many of his stories, unlike these two, are very funny indeed. There is a strong Yiddish tradition of poking fun at Jewish eccentricities.

ii. The Rebel

Albert Camus, member of the French resistance but in revolt against the mindless revolutionaries of our day, torn over Algeria, dying prematurely in a motor-car accident, is in some ways the representative intellectual man of our times – honest, empty of faith, passionate, hopeless, apostle of the existential absurdity of the human condition, and one leader, as Sir Herbert Read put it, of 'the revolt of man against the conditions of life, against creation itself'. Like Chazkele and the Rabbi of Bechev he shakes a fist at the universe. It is incomprehensible. It is absurd. There is a 'hopeless encounter between human questioning and the silence of the universe'. If the universe does not answer man's anguished questioning and everything, evil especially, becomes a painful enigma, what is to be done? Chazkele and Rabbi Nechemiah found answer only in dying. 'Not to be born is the best for man' they might have said.

Camus, on the other hand, affirms life. He recognises 'human life as the single necessary good'. Not only because it can be argued to be a good in itself, but because without it there would be no challenge to the universe, no one to ask the necessary questions (which are nevertheless 'hopeless' because they are not answered).

It is the slenderest possible ground for an ethical and social philosophy. Why should a *hopeless* questioning of an unanswering universe continue? Or even be necessary at all? Is that not an absurdity as great as life, and a thin consolation for so much suffering, particularly on the part of those who experience no impulse to question anything more profound than the cost of living? Whatever the case, Camus establishes his philosophy of the absurd in the very heart of contemporary moral humanism. He begins from the opposite pole to Chaz-

---

[2] *A Friend of Kafka,* p. 221.

[3] *Ibid.,* pp. 222–3.

[4] *Ibid.,* p. 283.

[5] *Ibid.,* p. 311.

kele and the Rabbi. They launch into their quest for meaning from deep within a religious context: Camus begins with an initial acceptance of the nothingness – the death, if you will, of God – and defends his position in a passage of Promethean defiance.

'The words which reverberate for us at the confines of this long adventure of rebellion, are not formulae for optimism, for which we have no possible use in the extremities of our unhappiness, but words of courage and intelligence which, on the shores of the eternal seas, even have the qualities of virtue.

'No possible form of wisdom today can claim to give more. Rebellion indefatigably confronts evil, from which it can only derive a new impetus. Man can master, in himself, everything that should be mastered. He should rectify in creation everything that can be rectified. *And after he has done so, children will still die unjustly even in a perfect society.* Even by his greatest effort, man can only propose to diminish, arithmetically, the sufferings of the world. But the injustice and the suffering of the world will remain and, no matter how limited they are, they will not cease to be an outrage. Dimitri Karamazov's cry of "Why?" will continue to resound through history: and rebellion will only die with the death of the last man on Earth.'[1]

Camus's fiction presents us with two characters who give opposing pictures of the emptiness of the universe and the hollowness of man. One is Jean-Baptiste Clamence, the judge-penitent of *The Fall,* and the other Mersault, the young murderer of *The Outsider.* Clamence begins with everything most men desire – wealth, status, good looks, success with women, Parisian life at its bourgeois best – and strips himself till he has nothing. Mersault begins with nothing and is stripped even of life itself. Clamence has asked for everything and received it to overflowing: Mersault expected nothing, asked nothing, except to be left alone: this one modest wish was not granted him. In the judge-penitent fable Clamence slowly realises his own hollowness and bad faith. His nausea for his own humbugging being (equal to Antoine Roquentin's in *La Nausée* by Jean-Paul Sartre) is completed when he allows a girl to drown without effort to save her: he is a coward and incapable of a living response to another being. On the other hand Mersault makes no response to his mother's death. He feels incapable of grief, and, for that matter, of hypocrisy. If he could have made the usual insincere noises of contrition over his mother's death and of repentance over the wanton and unpremeditated killing of which he stands accused, all might have been well. But he does not feel these things and is amazed that anyone should wish him to confess to something he does not feel.

The actual murder hardly now seems something which he *did*. It just *happened*. The heat glaring from the sands had been as fierce as an oven, sweat had almost blinded him, there was the flash of a knife. The murder belonged to these climatic and physiological crises, not to his will, not to his guilt. His destruction by guillotine becomes necessary to society in the story, not only because he is guilty, but because he is morally naked, emotionally numb, the true outsider.

The hollowness of such characters as Clamence and Mersault reflects for Camus the hollowness perceived in the universe itself. But not only by Camus. It surfaces again and again in modern literature as character after character asks, 'What is the meaning of it all?' or more religously, 'Where is redemption to be found?' or in the rabbi's words, 'Is something there?' These are the central questions of much contemporary fiction.

To pursue this through the travails of literary humanism in this century – for which the great question is whether the universe is hostile to man or not – would take a separate study. I will simply point to cries for help in contemporary writing which illustrate it.

[1]*The Rebel,* Hamilton, 1953, p. 27 – my italics

iii. *'Something is there'*
In *Another Country*[1] James Baldwin, that brilliant black American novelist, spells out for us the rootless life of the agnostic urban black and his shame-faced, sympathising

white intellectual friends in New York: the cruelty, the rapacity of the hard city are so omnipresent that they become unbearable to the reader. Never was a book on the situation of the blacks so hopeless in mood, and not alone about the blacks. What drives young Rufus Scott to suicide from the bridge at night is not only the humiliation of being a black, one born to wipe the spittle from his cheek, but the impossibility of being human. That impossibility is explored in terms that transcend race hatred. Rufus does not hate all whites, and some love him: many are his friends. To achieve communication first, and after that love between human beings is an enterprise in which men and women fail often than they succeed – 'and every success is a different kind of failure' – even where there is no colour complication. Rufus has the additional burden of being a homosexual, and this for him is an affront to his pride, a perversion of his given sexuality, a gross insult to his human dignity. He did not *ask* for any of these humiliations. Just to live is itself an injustice. What stays in the mind, and in a sense stops the book, making all after it an anti-climax, is young Rufus hurling himself from the bridge, in Oedipean rejection of his fate, weeping, blaspheming as he falls towards the God he does not believe in.

Another who will have no part in the world is Jimmy Porter in John Osborne's *Look Back in Anger*. It is true he does not commit suicide but storms along, lacerating others, the first male shrew on stage, swearing at his own self-laceration, striking out blindly in reply to mostly imaginary injuries, driving his bewildered and innocent wife from him. He suffers from the same world rejection as Rufus Scott. His sex and class war against his wife is to make her suffer as he suffers and when all possibility of communication with the wife he has destroyed seems lost, he bursts out:

'Was I really wrong to believe that there's some kind of burning virility of mind and spirit that looks for something as powerful as itself? The heaviest, strongest creatures in this world seem to be the loneliest, like the old bear following his own breath in the dark forest. There's no warm pack, no herd to comfort him. That voice that cries out doesn't *have* to be a weakling's, does it?'[2]

The same theme of anger at the human condition and the silence of the universe appears in David Storey's gothick novel *Radcliffe*, a novel of the power of which this gifted writer seems unaware. *Radcliffe* celebrates, with a steamy emotional genius worthy of *Wuthering Heights* – it is set in the same countryside – the collapse of a Northern family dynasty, the ruin of a noble house, and the murder of one psychotic homosexual by another. But when the murderer Radcliffe is tried, he seeks to justify his torrid crime by philosophising about the split in European consciousness, brazenly arguing a Platonic justification of homosexuality as a power which creates order in society. Counsel accuses Radcliffe of hiding his own sense of guilt behind the accusation of a general corruption of society. He feverishly denies this but when asked why then he killed his friend, he replies that it was because whatever they touched they destroyed.

When this failed to satisfy counsel Radcliffe 'turned away. He seemed senseless. "Oh God," he cried, shaking his fist at the court, "I wanted something huge and absolute! I wanted an absolute! I wanted an ideal! I wanted an order for things!"'[3]

When the ideal, the absolute, cannot be found the only answer this literary tradition comes up with is the fist shaken at the universe, the impulse to destroy everything. It is a powerful nihilist literary tradition with writers like Jean-Paul Sartre, Jean Genet, Norman Mailer, William Burroughs typical of it. It is the sort of pabulum on which many young terrorists fed.[4]

The prevailing secular view of the world is an empty and pessimistic one. The expanding universe is, they say, the consequence of an explosion, apparently random, for no one can guess at its causation. It just happened. Our planet was an accident too. Life on it was the product of pure chance and the emergence of man at the end of a long and intricate evolutionary chain was purposeless too. It is a universe without room for reason, order, design, perhaps indeed for love or hate. So one could reasonably conclude.

Man finds himself an alien in this dense, uncomprehending material universe, and that is a source of grief. But where does *grief* come from? How could there be any such thing if the universe is senseless? What is the source of the rage of Chazkele and the Rabbi of Bechev against poverty, persecution, cruelty and terror? These very words have absolutely no meaning in a universe which apparently *accidentally* threw up man. Nothing in *the universe* makes moral protest when the fly perishes in the stomach of the spider. In that sense the universe is amoral. But *man* makes protest, feels anguish to the point of self-destruction, at the failures and evils of himself and others. 'Failures and evils'! This is the discourse of man again, not of the universe. Did man just invent it (at random)? It does not make sense. If man *belongs* to his universe 'something' must echo within it that which surfaces in man as his most noble nature – such gifts as love, sacrifice, honour, justice, mercy. These are not the meaningless words so much contemporary fiction supposes, or presupposes. Much of the rage against man and god we have been exploring is in fact inspired because man does not *honour* these words as he should and God does not compel him – or they believe, and mourn the fact, that there is no God to compel him. In terms of a materialist universe those 'words' have no meaning. In terms of the human spirit they are everything. For the Bible they are the godly gifts of the divine Spirit, the speech of angels.

'But the harvest of the Spirit,' St Paul wrote in Galatians (5: 22–25) 'is love, joy, peace, patience, kindness, goodness, fidelity, gentleness, and self-control. There is no law dealing with such things as these. And those who belong to Christ Jesus have crucified the lower nature with its passions and desires. If the Spirit is the source of our life, let the Spirit also direct our course.'

'Something is there', the Rabbi of Bechev murmured as he lay dying and ended his war with God.

> 'The people who walked in darkness
>   have seen a great light:
> light has dawned upon them,
>   dwellers in a land as dark as death.'

Thus the Bible's book of Isaiah, and later:

> 'I, I myself, am he that comforts you.
> Why then fear man, man who must die,
>   man frail as grass?
>   Why have you forgotten the Lord your maker,
> who stretched out the skies and founded the earth?
>   Why are you continually afraid, all the day long,
> why dread the fury of oppressors ready to destroy you?
>   Where is that fury?
> He that cowers under it shall soon
>   stand upright and not die . . .'
> (9:2 & 51:13–14)

[1] Dial 1962; Michael Joseph 1963.

[2] *Op. cit.,* Faber and Faber 1957, p.94.

[3] *Radcliffe* by David Storey, Longmans 1963, p. 371.

[4] Cf. *Hitler's Children* by Jillian Becker, Michael Joseph 1977.

6: 'Go Tell It on the Mountain'

i. 'How glorious is thy name'

Go Tell It on the Mountain[1] is the title, drawn from the famous hymn,[2] of another of James Baldwin's novels. It concerns black homespun religion in the black secular city. What shines out so brightly in that book is not only the fierce faith and real joy of the tiny storefront congregation – a faith which we see (and see why) made of the ex-slaves a great and enduring *people* – but the precariousness, even the hollowness of this Christian stand in the face of changes in black consciousness and the pressures of a great indifferent city slamming itself into the air around the storefront church in Harlem. These people, poor and underprivileged, wrestle with Satan, and wrestle with God with a sweating passion that has all the heat and abandon of the sinful lusts they seek to savage away in their own bodies.

'They sang with all the strength that was in them, and clapped their hands for joy. There had never been a time when John had not sat watching the saints rejoice with terror in his heart, and wonder. Their singing caused him to believe in the presence of the Lord; indeed, it was no longer a question of belief, because they made that presence real. He did not feel it himself, the joy they felt, yet he could not doubt that it was, for them, the very bread of life – could not doubt it, that is, until it was too late to doubt. Something happened to their faces and their voices, the rhythm of their bodies, and to the air they breathed; it was as though wherever they might be became the upper room, and the Holy Ghost were riding on the air.'[3]

A 'saved' young boy danced. Elisha 'cried out, *Jesus, oh Lord Jesus!* He struck on the piano one last, wild note, and threw up his hands, palms upward, stretched wide apart. The tambourines raced to fill the vacuum left by his silent piano, and his cry drew answering cries. Then he was on his feet, turning, blind, his face congested, contorted with this rage, and the muscles, leaping and swelling in his long, dark neck. It seemed that he . . . could not contain this passion, that he would be, before their eyes, dispersed into the waiting air. Sometimes he did not stop until he fell – until he dropped like some animal felled by a hammer – moaning, on his face. And then a great moaning filled the church.'[4]

The hero of the story, John, a black boy, just 15, goes through a night of screaming, tears and terror, before the altar and the praying, shouting congregation of the saints, as he makes his descent into the pit of hell before he is lifted up and 'his drifting soul was anchored in the love of God; in the rock that endures forever'. It is a story that is told not only beautifully but as passionately as the Pentecostalist faith itself is lived against the background of the very human sins and failures even of the self-same preachers who urge everyone into repentance. Then too there are the family strains brought on by the rebellion of the young against the tyranny of the fathers. Even John is torn between longing for salvation and damnation, between hatred for his stepfather and love of the eternal Father. It is a novel written in fire.

The rebellion against God, at which we have looked so carefully in the last chapter, creates an unhappy darkness even when it is conducted from the best of motives – compassion for the world's victims, or the search for 'progress' or 'enlightenment' or the demand for 'truth' even though it kills us. It produces a despair, even a numbness of the spirit, as though if God is dead, or never was, what now can be said about man and his unique place in the universe? That he is totally alone and without support – 'Nothing is there' – and must go it alone until the final extinction? This was Bertrand Russell's stoical and pessimistic philosophy, though he belied it in the way he lived for good causes. James Baldwin charts that desert sensitively in many works.

Certainly my last chapter was full of darkness, even death. But the Bible does not only speak of the rebellion against God, and rage against it, but of the love, the glory of God, the rejoicing in God, the sense that a God-given world is full of wonder, beauty, love and hope. The Old Testament and the

New burn with the dazzling presence of God, of the bright promise of Messianic hope, even of the splendour to which men are marching after death.

> O Lord our sovereign.
> how glorious is thy name in all the earth!
> Thy majesty is praised high as the heavens.
> Out of the mouths of babes, of infants at the breast,
>   thou hast rebuked the mighty . . .
>
> (Psalm 8)
>
> Come! Let us raise a joyful song to the Lord,
> a shout of triumph to the Rock of our salvation.
> Let us come into his presence with thanksgiving,
> and sing him psalms of triumph.
> For the Lord is a great God,
> a great king over all gods;
> the farthest places of the earth are in his hands,
>   and the folds of the hills are his;
> the sea is his, he made it;
> the dry land fashioned by his hands is his.
> Come! Let us throw ourselves at his feet in homage,
> let us kneel before the Lord who made us . . .
>
> (Psalm 95)

This overflowing gratitude for a world of loveliness, for a comely mankind and a God on the side of the men he created in his image is as much the mood of the New Testament as of the Old, especially in the Canticles. Mary cries out in the immortal Magnificat:

> Tell out, my soul, the greatness of the Lord,
> rejoice, rejoice, my spirit, in God my saviour.

And the contribution of the church itself in hymns, music, liturgy and art to this rejoicing is magical and past excelling. 'Rejoice in the Lord always, and again I say, rejoice', is the theme of a moving Purcell anthem, Handel's glorious *Messiah* typifies the magnificence of human worship.

All writers on the New Testament contrast the darkness of the days of the Passion in Jerusalem with the sweetness and light of the mission of Jesus on the flowering hills of Galilee among the peasants and children, where Jesus appears as a poet as well as a healer. Then, even though the Passion was so dark, by Pentecost only 50 days later the disciples were in such a mood of exaltation that men thought they were drunk at nine o'clock in the morning. And when we come to the Revelation of John, men are so intoxicated with the expectation of the kingdom that they are seeing visions of a new heaven, and a new earth. Even *heaven* is to be refashioned.

Far cry though it is, we have to ask – is there a note of joy and rejoicing in the kind of contemporary literature we have been looking at? There is plenty of sombreness, of world-weariness, of tragedy, but what of courage and grace and innocence among all those books? The judge-penitent in Camus's *The Fall* speaks of those 'who have lost track of the light, the mornings, the holy innocence of those who forgive themselves'. That could be all of us. It certainly describes many, many writers for whom the world is without hope. Both Saul Bellow and Graham Greene for instance write and perhaps live in the sadness of this defeat. Even so it may be unfair to single them out, except that they are representative as well as famous.

What has gone out of the world and out of literature too is the sense, the sensation of *glory*. The Rev Kenneth Greet, writing in *The Guardian,*[5] said:

'If we looked for glory it would rekindle our hope. "I don't know what you mean by glory," Alice said in *Through the Looking Glass*. "I meant, there's a nice knock-down argument for you," replied Humpty. And he was right. All the words of all the preachers may fail to make God real to me or dispel my despair. But show me a glimpse of glory, and that will do it.'

The metaphysical poet, Henry Vaughan, glimpsed it in a famous passage[6] –

I saw Eternity the other night
Like a great Ring of pure and endless light,
  All calm, as it was bright,
And round beneath it, Time in hours, days, years
  Driv'n by the spheres
Like a vast shadow mov'd, In which the world
  And all her train were hurl'd . . .

and the rest of the poem conjures up the struggle of man to escape the 'thick midnight fog' of his sick world and to follow those who singing and weeping 'soar'd up into the Ring' of glory which led to God.

> A way where you might tread the Sun, and be
>   More bright than he . . .

We can find among modern poets too the same innocence and joy. It caused Anne Ridler to ask whether

> . . . this body loved so
> In its young crocus light, and the full orb of manhood,
> And the paean of sound, all that our senses know
> Is not the matter of God?[7]

Gerard Manley Hopkins, full of passionate worship of a shining, blessed, God-haunted world sang of Jesus –

> I kissed my hand
> To the stars, lovely as under
> Starlight, wafting him out of it; and
> Glow, glory in thunder;
> Kiss my hand to the dappled-with-damson west:
> Since, tho' he is under the world's splendour and wonder,
> His mystery must be instressed, stressed
> For I greet him the days that I meet him, and bless when I understand.[8]

This blitheness of spirit blossomed in Dylan Thomas's 'Fern Hill' that evocative poem of his childhood.

> Now as I was young and easy under the apple boughs
> About the lilting house and happy as the grass is green.

and mounted to an impassioned declaration in 'And death shall have no dominion'.[9]

And death shall have no dominion.
Dead men naked they shall be one
With the man in the wind and the west moon:
When the bones are picked clean and clean bones gone,
They shall have stars at elbow and foot,
Though they go mad they shall be sane,
Though they sink through the sea they shall rise again.
Though lovers be lost, love shall not;
And death shall have no dominion.

The passion is there again in T. S. Eliot (not noticeably a passionate man) in the famous lyric from his 'Little Gidding'.[10]

The dove descending cleaves the air
With flame of incandescent terror
Of which the tongues declare
The one discharge from sin and error.

Flame? Incandescence? Such gifts are rare among contemporary prose writers (though we might well exempt C. S. Lewis in *Surprised by Joy* and study with profit H. A. Williams's *The Joy of God*) if we mean by them, not only superb prose, but a breakthrough of the spirit in joy and hope despite the tormented world.

[1]Knopf, 1953; Michael Joseph, 1954.

[2]The words are by Geoffrey Marshall Taylor. The refrain runs
    Go, tell it on the mountain,
    Over the hills and everywhere,
    Go, tell it on the mountain,
    That Jesus is His name.
The source is Isaiah 52:7 –
    'How lovely on the mountains are the feet of the herald
    who comes to proclaim prosperity and bring good news,
        the news of deliverance.'

[3]*Op. cit.*, pp. 15–16.

[4]*Ibid*, pp. 16–17.

[5]April 7, 1979.

[6]Henry Vaughan, 1621–95. The poem 'The World' is from *Works*, ed. L. C. Martin, 1914.

[7]'Crammer and the Bread of Heaven'. From *A Matter of Life and Death,* Faber and Faber 1959.

[8]*The Poems of Gerard Manley Hopkins,* Oxford 3rd ed. 1948, p. 5 'The Wreck of the Deutschland.'

[9]Dylan Thomas, *Collected Poems, 1934–1952,* Dent 1952, p. 68.

[10]Fourth of 'The Four Quartets'. *The Complete Plays and Poems of T. S. Eliot,* Faber and Faber 1969, p. 191 *et seq.*

ii. Matryona's House

One of the few stories of pure joy that I know is a short story by Tibor Dery, a Hungarian writer, simply called 'Love'.[1] It tells of a political prisoner who has served seven years, one and a half of them in a condemned cell, suddenly and unexpected released and coming home, trembling and humble, to reunion with his wife and son. The delicate explosion of love and tenderness which follows their reunion simply cannot be illustrated by a quotation, such is the economy by which it is told. It is a story of grace and truth, sufficient in its brevity to be a new Testament parable.

Morning by Julian Fane[2] has the same quality of tremulous wonder and fundamental innocence. It is the story of a little boy growing up in a beautiful house and gardens to discovery of himself and other people in a world already under the shadow of war and it ends with his departure to a prep school. 'Everything is changed. He thinks of Nanny and Flora, then of sheep, shepherd, trees and pale blue sky, of all he sees, all he has known and may ever know – and he is not afraid.' This too is a work of incandescence.

I find this spirituality in Alexander Solzhenitsyn, not because of the quality of his Russian prose, which I cannot judge, but because of his Christian moral fervour, product of what other centuries would have called his years of martyrdom. He believes passionately in the high vocation of the writer to tell the truth, which will prevail.

In his Nobel Prize address[3] he quotes a Russian proverb, 'One word of truth is of more weight than all the rest of the world' and speaks of the constant encouragement he has received from his 'living feeling for *world literature* as one great heart, beating in response to the cares and troubles of our world, even though these are seen and presented in a different way in every different country.'[4]

One might have used *One Day in the Life of Ivan Denisovich, First Circle* or *Cancer Ward* to illustrate his power in the novel of high seriousness but I have chosen instead a simple short story, *Matryona's House*[5], because it has at its heart a peasant woman of incandescent goodness – Matryona. The story has struck with awe and delight all those Russians who have been able to read it, because Matryona lives and represents for them the immemorial Russia whose image has been defaced by an infamous regime. She belongs to a past which now begins to look more wholesome than the present. Matryona is alone. Her husband has never returned from the war; 'she had had six children, all of whom died, one after another, very early, so that no two were ever alive at the same time. Later there was a sort of foster daughter, Kira'. Matryona was old, she was often ill, she had to rest much on 'her wretched, raggedy bed' by the Dutch stove which was the sole source of heat in her one-room old house, slipping on its foundations. The *kolkhoz* or collective farm which determined everything in the village had not enrolled her because of her ill-health. So she did not get paid. Nevertheless it dictated to her just as if she were a member and called upon her for 'voluntary services'.

The narrator, a schoolmaster just appointed to the village school (obviously Solzhenitsyn himself) has come in from exile in Asiatic lands and is enchanted to find a real old village where the Russian he loves is spoken and he feels he has found his birthright again as he breathes the forest air. He asks to lodge with her in that one-roomed hovel so typical of Russian rural poverty. His contribution to her income is valuable. But he has to share her poverty – milk from the one goat and two gruel meals a day. Old and poor nevertheless she helps everybody and they all call upon her in emergencies. She never expects pay. It seems wrong to her. She is a village institution.

It turned out too that her husband, Yefim, abandoned her for drink and a mistress even before the Army took him. 'She dresses any old way and always looks like a hick', he is reported to have said, and the narrator says of her, 'She never tried to acquire things for herself. She wouldn't struggle to buy things which then mean more to her than life itself . . . Her moral and ethical standards made her a misfit. She was considered "odd" by her sisters and her sisters-in-law – a laughing stock – because, as they said, she was so stupid as to work for others without pay. She never accumulated property against the time of her death when her only possessions were a dirty white goat, a crippled cat, and rubber plants . . .'[6]

She does not just *die* in the course of the story – she is killed helping her relatives. The circumstances are these. Her step-daughter, Kira is married. She and her husband have been offered a plot of land not far away on condition that they erect a dwelling on it. Matryona possessed a *gornitsa* – a small annex – to her one-roomed cottage. It is promised to Kira, who now comes to claim it through her father. But they have to take it down stealthily and move it by night before the *kolkhoz* officials get wind of what is happening. They pile the stuff in two ramshackle sledges and pull it away with a 'borrowed' tractor. Matryona fears they may break down and hurries unnecessarily to help. What help can *she* give, poor old soul, who in surrendering the *gornitsa* had done all and more than could be asked of her?

One sledge breaks down on the railway line and an unlighted train crashes into it. The 'helping' Matryona and Kira's brother-in-law are killed.

Vultures gather round to claim what they can of Matryona's poor belongings.

'We all lived beside her,' the narrator comments, 'and never understood that she was that righteous one without whom, according to the proverb, no village can stand.

'Nor any city.

'Nor our whole land.'

[1]Tibor Dery, *The Giant*, John Calder 1964, p. 125 *et seq.*

[2]John Murray 1956.

[3]Alexander Solzhenitsyn, *Nobel Prize Lecture,* transl. Nicholas Bethell, Stenvalley Press, 1973.

[4]*Op. cit.*, p. 47.

[5]First published in *Novymir*, the prestigious Russian literary review, in 1963.

[6]Alexander Solzhenitsyn, *We Never Make Mistakes*, Sphere 1972, p. 89.

iii. Morning Tide

Matryona calls to mind another mother from a forgotten novel, *Morning Tide*, by Neil M. Gunn.[1] Forgotten, yes, but that is sad for it is a work of pure genius. It is the story of a dying fishing community in Caithness in Scotland, where the old values for which Matryona stood still hold the community together – the comradeship of the small fishing fleet, the life of the Kirk, the daily presence of poverty which neighbourliness makes bearable. The sense that the community must disintegrate under modern commercial pressures and that the old values will crack is omnipresent and is being faced with courage as well as resignation. The same destiny faced Matryona's community. However, the sense of Christian loss is not as strong in *Morning Tide* as in *Matryona's House* for the Caithness village teems with joy and vigour, the more as it is seen through the eyes of a barefoot boy, Hugh, who storms through his own and other people's crises, including the emigration of his only, much-loved brother to Australia and a loved, lovely sister to London.

Of Hugh's mother, who is facing death from heart trouble, his sister Kirsty says: ' "Often when mother has been sitting alone by the fire, I would come upon her unbeknown, and would look at her and wonder what she was thinking. You have seen her like that. And then when she knew you were there she would look round and smile. She was always so pleased to see you then. There was nothing ever sad or sorrowful about mother. She was never like the wifies who go about mourning at the Communion times. Have you ever thought about it, Hugh, that mother was never very religi-ous? And yet –" Kirsty's low voice came with a rush of conviction – "I would sooner have her mind than all the religions of the world! Oh, Hugh, mother was so quiet and wise. She did not cry, Lord! Lord! – she knew . . . Sometimes when I'm away from mother, I see her, Hugh, not so much like our mother, but like a woman . . . like a woman sitting alone . . . and going back and going back and going back . . . she is like a great mother of great peoples . . .

' "You know, away in the time of the Preacher and in those strange places, mother would be a woman amongst them wise and calm, smiling and hospitable and welcoming them. Our mother. She would. In some ways the world here is little, and the people are little. We are all – I don't know – we seem to be passing away. And these wifies who go moaning about their religion – they don't understand the greatness of her spirit." '[2]

The crises which Hugh witnesses and shares in with the crystal sharp vision of childhood, which is poetry itself, are many. Among them is the great storm which rages through the village and catches the tiny fleet at sea. 'The noise of the sea rose above all other sounds, rose high up over the earth from a far booming source, a thunder of doom . . . The solid earth trembled.' Hugh and his sister fight their way down to the harbour in the dark before dawn, to discover what they can, in a danger which threatens them too, because their brother Alan is part of the crew of one boat and their father is skipper of another. They face the sea, two frail young things, as the dawn comes. 'Out of the murk each roller came, a wall of water, deliberately gathering volume, massing itself, stead-ily advancing, gaining speed, curling all along the line to a smoking crest, onrushing, uprising – till its baffled speed thundered crest-first on the beach. . . But already, behind, the new wave was gathering volume, massing itself . . .'

The boats ride in through the impossible storm. One is smashed on the piles of the harbour mouth, though the crew are saved. Alan and his father come through, though Alan nearly drowns rescuing a man. Both are heroes to young Hugh shivering, inwardly praying, turned almost to ice in thin clothes by the power of the gale. Caithness is a stern biblical community, unwilling and unused to displaying its feelings, and both Hugh and Kirsty have to hide their tears of gratitude for the saving of brother and father. They have the problem again when brother Alan and sister Grace are given a village send-off at the bus station. Their emotions choke them. There are other moments of superb understanding of nature and of the feelings of men and women, young and old when Hugh, all on his own, snatch-hooks a grilse from a rocky hill pool, and stuffs it under his jersey and hiding from the keepers in a wood on his way home involuntarily witnesses the tender love-making of his sister Kirsty. How subtly this is all done!

It is on the way home from these escapades that he learns that his mother is dying from her tired old heart. There seems no hope. He calls for Kirsty, and, mocked by other boys, runs till exhausted for the doctor. He sits up with his mother to whom Kirsty reads the Bible – those resigned beautiful passages from Ecclesiastes such as:

'I returned, and saw under the sun, that the race is not to the swift, nor the battle to the strong, neither yet bread to the wise, nor yet riches to men of understanding, nor yet favour to men of skill; but time and chance happeneth to them all . . .'

It is after this reading that Kirsty speaks of her new understanding of their mother as an integral, saintly religious person. 'I know what religion is now' she said to Hugh, half-wondering, half-searching, and in love with her vision. In the end, the exhausted Hugh falls asleep to be woken in the dawn with the news that his mother is better.

Eventually he escapes outside from the embarrassment of his joy. A sense of 'exquisite motion got into Hugh's body. He wanted to run . . . He blew the air noisily through his lips, and trampled the earth in dancing steps. The round rusted end of a little tin a stone's throw away caught his eye. Picking up a pebble, he let fly, and hit the tin, making it give a ludicrous jump. Thrilled by the unexpected accuracy, he crouched under the sound. His mother would have heard that. Embarrassment made him blush. His mouth fell open as he listened. The lances of the new morning came about him and he challenged their leaping ecstasy, his eyes flashing hither and thither in his still head as he thought of his mother who had been given up for dead but was alive and would be wondering at this moment what he was doing knocking tins about. When he would go in at the door in a minute, she would call him! . . . Unless he went to the woods – for an offering? His head turned. And all at once he started running, his body light and fleet, his bare legs twinkling across the fields of dawn.'[3]

Well, there is the joy we have been searching for, the ecstasy of resurrection morning, the sense that because death has been overcome the new day opens. We can share through such works the joy of God when he looked upon his creation and saw that it was good.

Of course Neil Gunn is not alone in recreating for us that biblical rejoicing in a world made new for us each morning. Something of that sense comes through in many works. I may instance one or two – Victor Gollancz's *Letter to Timothy*, Frank Kendon's *The Small Years*, Siegfried Sassoon's *Memoirs of a Fox-Hunting Man*, Richard Church's *Over the Bridge*, Laurie Lee's *Cider with Rosie*, an especially beautiful evocation, and a cult book, and of course *Le Grand Meaulnes* by Alain-Fournier, which is also a cult book. All of these, except the last, perhaps, must be regarded as autobiographies. Is it an accident that it is when childhood is being written about that joy and innocence and glory in life and the world reveal themselves? No, no accident. There is a childhood vision and intensity of feeling which sees everything in a peculiar light before years and experience tarnish the days, and the shades of the prison-house close.

Thomas Traherne caught this more beautifully than any writer in his *Centuries of Meditation* – and long before Wordsworth – where he as a child snatched at the immortality of things seen for the first time.

'The corn was Orient and Immortal Wheat, which never should be reaped, nor was ever sown. I thought it had stood from everlasting to everlasting. The dust and stones of the street were as precious as gold: the gates were at first the end of the world. The green trees when I saw them first through one of the gates transported and ravished me, their sweetness and unusual beauty made my heart to leap, and almost mad with ecstasy, they were such strange and wonderful things. The men! O what venerable and reverend creatures did the aged seem! Immortal cherubims! And young men glittering and sparkling angels, and maidens strange seraphic pieces of life and beauty! Boys and girls tumbling in the street, and playing, were moving jewels. I knew not that they were born or should die; but all things abided eternally as they were in their proper places. Eternity was manifest in the light of the day, and something infinite behind everything appeared: which talked with my expectation and moved my desire . . . So that with much ado I was corrupted, and made to learn the dirty devices of this world. Which now I unlearn, and become, as it were, a little child again that I may enter into the kingdom of God.'[4]

We all know what St Matthew wrote:

'At that time the disciples came to Jesus and asked, "Who is the greatest in the kingdom of Heaven?" He called a child, set him in front of them, and said, "I tell you this: unless you turn round and become like children, you will never enter the kingdom of Heaven. Let a man humble himself till he is like this child, and he will be the greatest in the kingdom of Heaven. Whoever receives one such child in my name receives me." '

'Eternity was manifest in the light of day, and something infinite behind everything appeared', Thomas Traherne said.

'Something is there', said the Rabbi Nechemiah.

'And the *Word* was God,' said St John.

[1] The Porpoise Press (Edinburgh) 1931.

[2] *Op. cit.*, pp. 278–9.

[3] *Op. cit.* p. 287.

[4] *Centuries of Meditation* by Thomas Traherne, Dobell 1934, Third Century, no. 3, p. 152.

Index of writers and titles